AWAK

AWAKE MY SOUL

Reflections on Thirty Hymns

J. R. Watson

First published in Great Britain in 2005

Society for Promoting Christian Knowledge
36 Causton Street
London SW1P 4ST

British Library Cataloguing-in-Publication Data
A catalogue record for this book is available from the British Library

ISBN 0-281-05768-0

1 3 5 7 9 10 8 6 4 2

Typeset by Graphicraft Ltd, Hong Kong
Printed in Great Britain by Bookmarque Ltd,
Croydon, Surrey

Contents

God's World: Pilgrimage and Thankfulness   111

God's People: Prayer and Dedication   135

To Frank Whitehead

Introduction

My original working title for this book was *Verses that Find Us*. I was thinking of the way in which hymns enter into our minds and hearts; 'find' us, as George Herbert put it:

> A verse may find him, who a sermon flies,
> And turn delight into a sacrifice.

These words not only contain a deep truth – that poetry and hymns can sometimes touch us in the way that doctrine does not – but they are also important in the history of hymn writing, because they gave permission to poets who had been somewhat doubtful about writing on sacred subjects. If the saintly Mr George Herbert thought that verse could be good for the soul, and if Bishop Ken could write his morning and evening hymns, the way was open for the great flood of hymnody which followed in the eighteenth century and after. Herbert saw that people liked poems better than sermons: he knew that people who 'fled' from sermons might take delight in poems or hymns.

And so it is. For most people, hymns have always been the part of a service that they like best. There are a number of reasons for this, apart from the fact that sermons can sometimes be dull or uninspiring. The first is that hymn singing is, for the most part, a joyful activity. It is the congregation's turn to play a part in the service, and it is always more pleasant to be an active participant than a passive spectator. It is enjoyable to stand up and sing, the body and voice expressing the feelings, working with the mind to register praise and prayer.

It is a joy, too, to share that singing with others, to know the sense of unity that comes when a congregation sings a hymn that it knows well and likes. In singing hymns, the individual becomes part of a larger whole, a number of people whose hearts and voices are all moving in the same direction. Together, those people sing

1

of thankfulness, or hope, or dedication, or love; and in the process they grow closer to each other. They become part of a society, the congregation at praise and prayer, and part of a greater congregation beyond that, the whole Church throughout the world, what John Ellerton called the 'Church unsleeping':

> As o'er each continent and island
> The dawn leads on another day,
> The voice of prayer is never silent,
> Nor dies the strain of praise away.

Beyond that is a greater congregation still, that of the communion of saints. We sing on earth in company with those in heaven: we can all remember our parents or grandparents having a favourite hymn, or singing hymns that they loved. To sing those hymns again is to be reunited with them for a moment, as they sing with us, but upon another shore and in a greater light. And beyond them stretch the generations of the past, legions of the known and unknown, the innumerable company of the heavenly host itself.

And certainly there are times when the singing of hymns becomes more than just a matter of words set to music. Often we sing dutifully and reverently; sometimes reluctantly, if we find something in the hymns that we do not like. But there are also moments in which the words and the music join to make something that is beyond our normal understanding: a hymn can take a congregation and lift it to heights of joy and inspiration that are seldom felt elsewhere. A hymn can be overwhelming in its power: there is a description of the congregation in St Paul's Cathedral at the third Lambeth conference in 1888, singing 'The Church's one foundation': 'It made them feel weak at the knees, their legs trembled, and they really felt as though they were going to collapse.'

Of course hymn singing is hardly ever like that. But its power to move and exalt is known to all who have sung a great hymn on a great occasion. It is known, too, to those who have sung a hymn in a small group, reverently and intensely, feeling the power of the words through the quietness of the singing. For hymns are wonderfully adaptable. They serve all occasions, from national thanksgivings to intimate gatherings of the faithful. This is because, at their best, they speak to the heart, to what Wordsworth called 'the human heart by which we live':

> Thanks to the human heart by which we live,
> Thanks to its tenderness, its joys, and fears,
> To me the meanest flower that blows can give
> Thoughts that do often lie too deep for tears.
> ('Ode. Intimations of Immortality from
> Recollections of Early Childhood')

Wordsworth was writing about nature, but for many people his words could be applied to the hymns that they love. They speak to the human heart, and they give thoughts that often lie too deep for tears, or for any of the usual registers of feeling. But they give us moments that we should cherish, for they transfigure the ordinariness of our normal lives.

It is in that transfiguration that hymns become most like poetry. I think that hymns *are* poems, usually: they perform the same function of stimulating our imagination and giving us a glimpse of that which we could not find in prose. Prose is the sermon; poetry is the hymn. The two complement one another, or should do, in a wonderfully satisfying mixture of thought and inspiration. In that process, hymns speak to our deepest needs: they call to us across the centuries, rich with an understanding of our hopes and fears. We all need reassurance: we are all conscious of our own failure and inadequacy, of the ways in which we have failed to live up to our aspirations, or to the hopes which others, and God, had for us. Hymns recognize those problems, help us to recognize them, assuage our fears, and speak to us of divine love.

They can speak to us of human love, too, and of the good society, 'the kingdom of God'. The topics of hymnody are almost inexhaustible. They bring us the Bible, with its great insights into individual spirituality and the good society, and its accounts of the life of Jesus. They apply these teachings – the law and the prophets from the Old Testament, the parables of justice and mercy from the New Testament – and relate them to our understanding of moral issues and individual development. They also speak to us of ourselves. Hymns can draw on all the features of our emotional and intellectual life: our joys and sorrows, our hopes and fears, our loves and hates.

And year by year we come to know them better and better. Hymns have an ongoing life within us, part of the life of the spirit which forms and shapes our every action, thought and feeling.

They become a part of us, something which we have in our memories and is a part of our lives. Herbert knew this: this is why he said, 'A verse may find him, who a sermon flies.' He knew that sometimes a verse 'finds' a person: it searches out the innermost needs of people, speaks to the inward self, ministers to the soul. A good hymn will do this. It will have a spiritual authenticity that comes from hard experience and a lively sympathy. When Isaac Watts says that 'Love so amazing, so divine, / Demands my soul, my life, my all', we can feel that he has thought long and deeply about the Passion of Christ; when Timothy Dudley-Smith writes 'Tell out, my soul, the greatness of the Lord', we can feel that he is saying to himself, '*These* are the words that I want to employ in the service of God.' It seems almost as if the words chose them, rather than the other way round: the words have inspired them, 'found' them, in Herbert's phrase, so that they can now 'find' us.

The 30 hymns in this collection are all, in my view, hymns that can work their particular magic upon us. I have written about them because I was asked to do so, but also as something of an experiment. These commentaries are very different from anything I have written before, which has been either historical or critical. There is very little reference here to the dates and circumstances of publication, or to textual matters such as omitted or altered verses. These may be found in the *Companion to Hymns and Psalms* (1988), which I edited with Kenneth Trickett and others, and *An Annotated Anthology of Hymns* (2002). Both books were historical, while *The English Hymn* (1997, 1999) was primarily the work of a literary critic. I remain convinced that these matters, and those that are literary and critical, are important; I think, in common with the orthodox critical axiom, that form and meaning are inseparable. But in this book I have tried to do something which (for me) is more difficult: I have tried to leave aside historical and formal matters and *listen* to what the hymn is saying.

I am convinced that listening to hymns is one of the most important responses that we can make. But it requires exceptional qualities of ear and eye, and a particular willingness to surrender to what the hymn is saying. There are two pitfalls that I have tried to steer between: paraphrase on the one hand and preaching on the other. I shall not have avoided them entirely. Writing this kind of study means that inevitably I shall have sometimes ended up saying in my own words what I think the hymn writer is saying – the difference being that he or she said it far better than I ever could. I may also have ended up, at times, with what I do not want to produce: a fragment of a sermon. I can say only that these short commentaries are not trying to summarize and not trying to preach. They are the brief reflections of a hymn-lover: the result of attempting to listen to the text and to pass on what I have heard, in the hope that this will be of some use to others.

I should like to thank Kay Griffiths, Gordon Taylor, Kenneth Trickett and Pauline Watson, all of whom have helped me.

J. R. Watson
Durham, Easter 2005

The hymns could have been arranged alphabetically or chrono-logically, but I have decided to place them in an order which begins with a nod to the customary pattern of *Hymns Ancient and Modern*: Morning and Evening hymns; the Christian Year; the Communion of Saints; Holy Communion. Thereafter the 'General Hymns' of *Ancient and Modern* have been arranged as follows: God, as Father, Son and Holy Spirit; hymns of Pilgrimage and Thankfulness; and hymns of Prayer and Dedication. While this selection is far too short to claim with John Wesley in his 1780 *Collection* that this is 'a little body of experimental and practical divinity', I hope that this will give some structure to this anthology.

MORNING AND EVENING

Awake, my soul, and with the sun
Thomas Ken (1637–1711)

Awake, my soul, and with the sun
Thy daily stage of duty run;
Shake off dull sloth, and joyful rise
To pay thy morning sacrifice.

Redeem thy mis-spent time that's past,
And live this day as if thy last;
Improve thy talent with due care;
For the great day thyself prepare.

Let all thy converse be sincere,
Thy conscience as the noon-day clear;
Think how all-seeing God thy ways
And all thy secret thoughts surveys.

Wake, and lift up thyself, my heart,
And with the angels bear thy part,
Who all night long unwearied sing
High praise to the eternal King.

Glory to thee, who safe hast kept,
And hast refreshed me whilst I slept;
Grant, Lord, when I from death shall wake,
I may of endless light partake.

Lord, I my vows to thee renew;
Scatter my sins as morning dew;
Guard my first springs of thought and will,
And with thyself my spirit fill.

Direct, control, suggest, this day
All I design, or do, or say,
That all my powers, with all their might,
In thy sole glory may unite.

Praise God, from whom all blessings flow,
Praise him, all creatures here below;
Praise him above, angelic host,
Praise Father, Son, and Holy Ghost.

This is the 'Morning Hymn' by Bishop Thomas Ken, who wrote it for the scholars of Winchester College. Its companion is the lovely 'Evening Hymn', 'Glory to thee, my God, this night', and there was another one, the 'Midnight Hymn'. Ken was educated at Winchester College, and retained his connection with the school throughout his life; he was a Prebendary of Winchester Cathedral from 1680 to 1685, before becoming Bishop of Bath and Wells, from which he was ejected by becoming a 'non-juror', one who refused to swear the oath of allegiance to William III. He was a man of great principle and nobility of character, who saw his duty plain before him and strove always to do it; and something of that straightforwardness may be seen in these lines.

Ken's hymns were written for schoolboys, and they have about them a directness and simplicity that makes them easy to understand. The rhyming couplets often, though not always, contain a precept over two easily remembered lines:

Awake, my soul, and with the sun
Thy daily stage of duty run.

There is no waiting about here, no hesitation: the hymn begins with an imperative – 'Awake' – as though the very briskness of the writing reinforces the message. Wake up with the sun, it says: do your duty every morning. The first daily duty is morning prayers, followed by school work; Ken knows that schoolboys do not always concentrate, or work hard, so he urges them to 'Redeem thy mis-spent time that's past'. It is easy, as a schoolboy, to have no care for the future, to waste time and be idle, so Ken suggests that they should 'live this day as if thy last'. If we knew that this would be our last day on earth, how differently would we behave! Every second would be precious, and every minute would be packed with meaningful activity.

This leads Ken to think of judgement day. The parable of the talents (from Matthew 25.14–30) is one in which the servants who used the gifts that they were given and improved them are praised, and the unprofitable servant who hid his talent and left it unused is rebuked. So the boys are urged to improve their talents, and prepare themselves for the great day of judgement. If they do that, then their conversation should be sincere (no telling lies) and their conscience clear (no hiding wrongdoing); if they hide things from their fellow schoolboys and their masters, they need to remember that God sees everything.

So it is in the light of this severe set of precepts that the child is urged to awake. This is what he must have in his mind as he gets up – the resolve to do better ('could do better' used to be a common phrase in school reports) and the resolve to bear in mind that God sees everything. With this in mind, he is to awake and sing with the angels, who have never been asleep at all but have sung all night and are never tired.

Set out like this, the hymn seems impossibly strict. This is some high-minded preceptor, we might think, who has no sense of what boys are really like. And yet it is important for them to have an ideal of good conduct set before them. Very few school children could live up to this: but as Browning wrote: 'A man's reach should exceed his grasp / Or what's a heaven for?'

The second half of the hymn is the boy's morning prayer. It gives glory to God for a safe and refreshing night's sleep, and prays to go to heaven after death. It renews the child's vows to God, and asks for forgiveness: in a lovely image, it prays for the sins to be scattered like morning dew – there at the beginning of the morning, but dried away by the sun's rays. Then the prayer is for help in the inner life of the soul – 'my first springs of thought and will' – followed by the outer life – 'all I design, or do, or say'. The verse acts out the interaction between the child and God, beginning with a prayer to God to 'direct, control, suggest', then centring on the child – all he plans or does or says, and all his powers – and then moving back to God – 'In thy sole glory may unite'.

Every verse has this unobtrusive but beautiful artistry. Each one seems simple, but is perfectly adapted to what it wants to say. Nowhere is this more evident than in the final verse, the doxology – 'Praise God, from whom all blessings flow'. As James Montgomery said in the preface to *The Christian Psalmist* (1825):

> it appears so easy, that one is tempted to think hundreds of the sort
> might be made without trouble. The reader has only to try, and he

will quickly be undeceived, though the longer he tries, the more difficult he will find the task to be.

Montgomery also pointed out that the verse shows us God 'as the object of praise in every view': praise for his blessings; praise by every creature, both on earth and in heaven; and praise in each of the characters in which he has revealed himself – Father, Son and Holy Ghost.

This precise neatness and absolute clarity is one reason why Ken's hymn has survived, in spite of the impossibly high standards which it presents. But there are other reasons why it is so much loved. The first is that by inviting the schoolboy to use all his powers to the glory of God, Ken is showing him the greatest possible respect. He is treating the boy as someone to whom he can speak very seriously, and whom he can encourage and admonish. The second is that what applies to the schoolboy in Winchester College in the seventeenth century applies to Christians in any time or place. These are precepts that we can all learn from; and although we may never succeed in living up to them, they provide a model set of rules for the conduct of a good and holy life. When I was a student at the University of Glasgow, we used to pray for the university every Commemoration Day, asking that 'godliness and good learning may here flourish and abide'. Godliness and good learning is, I think, what Ken was thinking of in this hymn: it is not so bad an ideal for an educational institution to aim at, or for its members to try to live up to; or, indeed, for any of us to have in our minds, day by day.

New every morning is the love
John Keble (1792–1866)

New every morning is the love
Our wakening and uprising prove;
Through sleep and darkness safely brought,
Restored to life, and power, and thought.

New mercies, each returning day,
Hover around us while we pray;
New perils past, new sins forgiven,
New thoughts of God, new hopes of heaven.

If on our daily course our mind
Be set to hallow all we find,
New treasures still, of countless price,
God will provide for sacrifice.

Old friends, old scenes, will lovelier be,
As more of heaven in each we see:
Some softening gleam of love and prayer
Shall dawn on every cross and care.

We need not bid, for cloistered cell,
Our neighbour and our work farewell,
Nor strive to wind ourselves too high
For sinful man beneath the sky:

The trivial round, the common task,
Would furnish all we ought to ask, –
Room to deny ourselves, a road
To bring us daily nearer God.

Only, O Lord, in thy dear love
Fit us for perfect rest above;
And help us this and every day
To live more nearly as we pray.

The Christian Year, by John Keble, was published in 1827. It went on to become the most popular book of religious poetry ever written, going through edition after edition during the nineteenth century. For most of us, all that remains of it now are a few hymns, selected out of the many poems; but for much of a century it was a book which was an indispensable part of any Anglican household, as beloved as Watts's *Psalms of David* or Bunyan's *Pilgrim's Progress* were for nonconformists.

It was a book for the Church of England. It had a poem for every Sunday of the church's year, as those Sundays were observed in the Book of Common Prayer, and the poems were related to the Gospel, Epistle or Collect for the day; they were intended, Keble said, to bring the reader's feelings 'into more entire unison with those recommended and exemplified in the Prayer Book'. In particular they demonstrated a certain ideal of behaviour: the quotation on the title page was 'In quietness and confidence shall be your strength' (from Isaiah 30.15), and the poems were full of that quietness and confidence. Keble described them as exhibiting what he called 'that *soothing* tendency in the Prayer Book'.

Poems in which the chief desire is to soothe do not sound very exciting, and these are not. But it is good to be quiet and reflective sometimes, and Keble ministers to that feeling with great skill. It is important to remember that the nineteenth century was a time which many people who lived in it saw as restless, confused, distracted and (above all) 'feverish'. Matthew Arnold's poem 'The Scholar-Gipsy' tells the wandering scholar to 'fly our paths, our feverish contact fly!' Keble uses these poems to soothe the soul at a difficult time, much as a doctor might try to soothe a feverish patient.

These verses are extracted from the opening poem of *The Christian Year*, which is called 'Morning'. It has a quotation from Lamentations 3.22–3: 'His compassions fail not. They are new every morning.' The last three words give Keble an opening to this verse which allows him to expand on the word 'compassions', just as the book as a whole expounds and explains the Sunday texts in the Prayer Book. In this case, the reader is to think of the love of God which produces a new day – wakening, getting up, safely brought through the night and restored to life, and power, and thought. Every day these things happen to us, and we take them for granted: Keble reminds us of the daily miracles of life and light.

Morning prayer comes next: as we pray, we are surrounded by further signs of God's love. The mercies, in a beautiful image, 'hover around us', bringing the hope of sins forgiven and of the promise of heaven. Then, after prayers, come the day's affairs, and these occupy the poet's thought for the remainder of the poem. If we try to make everything that we do holy, we shall have our reward: friends and places will be more precious day by day, and if we have cares they will be lightened. And we should not seek to be too special: Keble cautions against the idea that in order to be good Christians we need to enter a monastery and be especially holy. We should not think that we have to leave behind our common humanity, our neighbours and our work. We are a part of the world, and we should not try to avoid that: everything that we do – the trivial round, the common task – should be quite enough to bring us closer to God. Keble is echoing William Law, who said in *A Practical Treatise upon Christian Perfection* (1726) that the religious life 'calls no one to a Cloister, but to a right and full performance of those duties, which are necessary for all Christians, and common to all States of Life'.

The poem is one in which we are comforted by being accepted for what we are. We can be ordinary, and still serve God. There is only one requirement: that we should try, as the last verse says, to live up to our prayers. That sounds simple, although of course it is very difficult: but Keble has given us such a tender comfort in the earlier verses that here it actually seems as if it might be possible. It is the secret of life, as Herbert saw in 'Teach me, my God and King': to live life in accordance with our prayers, and to see God in everything. Keble puts it very simply: help us, today and every day, this morning and every morning, to live like that. Every morning is a new start, a time in which we can resolve to do better than before. Every morning is one in which we awake to life and light, to the thought of sins forgiven through the mercy of God.

It is that mercy which makes all things possible. We are all ordinary sinful people – no better or worse than we should be – perhaps, but every day we have this new opportunity to wake up to friendship, and work, and the chance to begin afresh. Because, as the last verse tells us, the guiding force is 'thy dear love':

Only, O Lord, in thy dear love
Fit us for perfect rest above.

The final prayer is that God, in his love, will make us fit for heaven; we pray it each Christmas as we sing 'Away in a manger': 'and fit us for heaven, to live with thee there'. It is a prayer, which, in its simplicity, holds the key to life – and to death; which is what Keble's hymn does, so beautifully and gently. It reminds us of the truly important things, as we wake up every morning to the miracle of a new day.

Abide with me; fast falls the eventide

Henry Francis Lyte (1793–1847)

———◆◆◆———

Abide with me; fast falls the eventide;
The darkness deepens; Lord, with me abide!
When other helpers fail, and comforts flee,
Help of the helpless, O abide with me.

Swift to its close ebbs out life's little day;
Earth's joys grow dim, its glories pass away;
Change and decay in all around I see;
O thou who changest not, abide with me.

I need thy presence every passing hour;
What but thy grace can foil the tempter's power?
Who like thyself my guide and stay can be?
Through cloud and sunshine, Lord, abide with me.

I fear no foe, with thee at hand to bless;
Ills have no weight, and tears no bitterness.
Where is death's sting? Where, grave, thy victory?
I triumph still, if thou abide with me.

Hold thou thy cross before my closing eyes;
Shine through the gloom, and point me to the skies;
Heaven's morning breaks, and earth's vain shadows flee:
In life, in death, O Lord, abide with me!

This hymn was written by Henry Francis Lyte, who was the Perpetual Curate (or parish priest) of Brixham, the fishing village in Devon. He is said to have given a handwritten copy of the hymn to a relative on Sunday 5 September 1847, after preaching his last sermon there. He was already ill, and went to the south of France to try to recover, but died at Nice on 20 November. During the journey south he sent back amendments to the hymn, which suggests that it was still evolving in his mind, and that it was in many ways a response to the end of his life as a priest and the closeness of his own death.

There is another story: that it was written 20 years earlier, when Lyte was nursing a dying friend. Unless fresh evidence appears, we shall never know whether it was written in response to his friend's death or to the approach of his own. I suspect (though I have nothing except a 'hunch' to go on) that a poem of some kind on this theme was written in about 1827 but never published, and that it resurfaced in Lyte's mind 20 years later when he was ill himself, whereupon he rewrote it and gave it to the member of his congregation who was (in the account given by his daughter) a near relative. But it does not really matter. What is important is the way in which the hymn approaches the problem of death, which we all have to face sooner or later (Lyte himself was only 54 when he died). Death is the end of all that we know, of all the familiar earthly things. It is a journey to what Hamlet called 'the undiscover'd country, from whose bourn / No traveller returns'; and we may each of us need to pray for help as we contemplate our imminent end. If Lyte preached his last sermon on 5 September and died on 20 November, he must have realized that the end was not far off; that he might never see Brixham again, never see the faces of his beloved fisherfolk again, never see another spring in that corner of Devonshire. So giving the poem to his relative in the congregation was his way of saying farewell.

The beauty of the poem is in its evocation of evening, an evening by the seashore which Lyte must have known so well. As priest of a little town where the chief occupation was fishing, he would have known the importance of watching the sea and knowing the tide. The rhythms of daily life depended on knowing the time of high water and low water, and on the hours of daylight – long in summer, short in winter. In this hymn the darkness is deepening, and the tide is going out; the poet is alone and comfortless.

There is a mystery in this hymn. It concerns our feelings as we stand by the sea, watching the light fail. We feel small and human beside the great power of the sea itself, and we also recognize the way in which our little lives are like a short day in the light of God, to whom a thousand years are but as yesterday when it is past, and as a watch in the night (Psalm 90.4). As the evening comes, and the tide goes out, we can feel that the seascape is an emblem of our lives – the morning of our youth, the high tide of our powers in the years that follow, and then the afternoon of life and the evening of old age. There is some mysterious bond between people and the sea, especially between those who live beside the sea and the ever-changing sea itself. Dickens wrote about it in *David Copperfield*, describing the death of Barkis in chapter 30. Barkis lingers on his deathbed, and Daniel Peggotty explains to David:

> 'People can't die, along the coast,' said Mr Peggotty, 'except when the tide's pretty nigh out. They can't be born, unless it's pretty nigh in – not properly born, till flood. He's a-going out with the tide. It's ebb at half-arter three, slack water half-an-hour. If he lives till it turns, he'll hold his own till past the flood, and go out with the next tide.'

Barkis dies a little later: 'And, it being low water, he went out with the tide.' This very powerful moment, issuing from Dickens's poetic imagination, carries on from what Lyte had written, perhaps only a year or two earlier (*David Copperfield* dates from 1849 to 1850).

Lyte describes the evening coming in two phrases – 'fast falls the eventide' and 'the darkness deepens' – in that beautiful first verse, where the long lines seem reflective, thoughtful and sad. On either side of 'fast falls' and 'darkness deepens' is the prayer – 'Abide with me' . . . 'with me abide'. This is adapted from the description in chapter 24 of St Luke's Gospel of the two disciples on the road to Emmaus. In their sadness after the crucifixion of Christ they meet a stranger on the road, who explains to them the underlying purposes of God in the death of Jesus Christ. As they reach their house in Emmaus, they invite him in, because it is late: 'Abide with us: for it is toward evening, and the day is far spent.'

In Lyte's hymn, 'us' becomes 'me'. And what was a simple kindness – 'stay the night, because it is getting late' – becomes a prayer: 'Abide with me.' The context of that prayer is everything that has been implied in the first verse, which suddenly becomes explicit in verse 2: 'Swift to its close ebbs out life's little day.' The whole of our life becomes like a single day, with its morning, noon and evening. Now 'earth's joys grow dim, its glories pass away.' There is a very real sadness in this hymn, which is one reason why it is so effective. But mingled with that sadness is the prayer for comfort, for the presence of God. The steadiness of God is the message: in the ever-changing world, the world of times and seasons, of tides and the sea, there is one who never changes: 'O thou who changest not, abide with me.'

In contrast, the world is always changing: 'Change and decay in all around I see.' The hours pass, sometimes good and sometimes bad, like English weather, the clouds and the sunshine of verse 3: 'Through cloud and sunshine, Lord, abide with me.' What Lyte is doing here is contrasting the steadfastness of God with the changeable state of human life, and this is why the hymn is such a great one. It corresponds so closely to what we all feel: the shortness of human life, the helplessness which we all have in the face of approaching death, the inevitability of the coming of night or death, and the need for a comforting presence in the darkest hours. Verse 4, with its reference to the resurrection, indicates the way:

> Where is death's sting? Where, grave, thy victory?
> I triumph still, if thou abide with me.

Such a triumph is accompanied by a consciousness of human finality, the closing eyes of death, the gloom of the deathbed. But through that gloom shines the promise, so that the hymn concludes with a wonderful mixture of hope and prayer. From the evening of life we come to the morning of heaven, but we do so not with confidence so much as with a feeling expressed in lines that sum up all that has gone before – our anxious hope and our prayerful hope:

> Heaven's morning breaks, and earth's vain shadows flee;
> In life, in death, O Lord, abide with me!

The day thou gavest, Lord, is ended

John Ellerton (1826–93)

The day thou gavest, Lord, is ended,
    The darkness falls at thy behest;
To thee our morning hymns ascended,
    Thy praise shall sanctify our rest.

We thank thee that thy Church unsleeping,
    While earth rolls onward into light,
Through all the world her watch is keeping,
    And rests not now by day or night.

As o'er each continent and island
    The dawn leads on another day,
The voice of prayer is never silent,
    Nor dies the strain of praise away.

The sun that bids us rest is waking
    Our brethren 'neath the western sky,
And hour by hour fresh lips are making
    Thy wondrous doings heard on high.

So be it, Lord; thy throne shall never,
    Like earth's proud empires, pass away;
Thy kingdom stands, and grows for ever,
    Till all thy creatures own thy sway.

This hymn is often used at funerals, although it is not really a funeral hymn. It was written for a book about missionary work in an age when it was seen as a duty for Christians to go out to convert members of other religions to Christianity. It was first published in *A Liturgy for Missionary Meetings* in 1870, with a text adapted from 1 Chronicles 23.30, 'Their office was to stand every morning to thank and praise the Lord, and likewise at even.' Ellerton adapts this quotation to stand for all those who praise God, morning and evening, all over the world.

It begins with evening, and with Evensong. The day is over, and the praise of God 'shall sanctify our rest'. It will mark the passing of the day into night. But the first verse also remembers that 'To thee our morning hymns ascended', so that it suggests a pattern of a traditional religious life – morning prayer and evening prayer, Matins and Evensong. The mind pictures a church or chapel on a typical Sunday, with two services, often attended by the same people – devout, loyal, diligent to attend church, happy to praise God in the morning and again in the evening.

It is from this homely and simple idea that the hymn suddenly 'takes off'. It moves at the beginning of verse 2 from the ordinary to the amazing. The reader or singer, who has been in church during the first verse, is taken up into the air and given a wonderful vision of the whole earth: the local church of verse 1 is part of the whole Church around the world which is engaged in the same business of prayer and praise, which goes on for 24 hours a day, so that it is the 'Church unsleeping'. It is seen as if from a spacecraft, the world spinning as it moves through space, while from country to country it rolls onward into light. What is evening in one place is afternoon in another, and morning in another, as 'o'er each continent and island / The dawn leads on another day'. As these lines are sung, the imagination travels across the world, as if turning over a globe. So we see that the same sun which goes down on us is rising somewhere else; there it is time for morning service even as we go to bed.

The hymn makes an extraordinary use of maps and of time zones. One reason why it is so beloved must be that it appeals to the geographer that exists in us all: that part of us which is fascinated by different places and people, by the way in which different countries have different experiences and climates. Reginald Heber used this delight in another missionary hymn:

> From Greenland's icy mountains,
>   From India's coral strand,
> Where Afric's sunny fountains
>   Roll down their golden sand,

22

From many an ancient river,
From many a palmy plain,
They call us to deliver
Their land from error's chain.

Countries pass before our eyes in these hymns: continents and islands lie beneath our view, doing the same thing – prayer and praise – at different times. The imagination is stretched, lifted out of its ordinary experience. As Charles Lamb said when one of his friends went to China: 'China – Canton – bless us – how it strains the imagination and makes it ache!'

Ellerton's hymn does not make the imagination ache so much as make it rejoice. It takes us on a swift journey across the world, charting the Church at praise, only to set us down safely again at the end. The last verse brings us back to where we began: it is as though the three middle verses had been a flying dream, from which we suddenly awake: 'So be it, Lord.' I like to think of the hymn as structured like a bridge, with three flying arches in the middle, anchored on either side by two solid abutments. The second of these, the final verse, awakens us from the dream to a reflection on that dream: Ellerton asserts that one day the missionary movement will ensure that the church grows and grows, 'till all thy creatures own thy sway'.

That last line reminds us that this hymn was written at the height of enthusiasm for Christian missions. All over the world dedicated men and women went out to convert people to belief in Jesus Christ as their Lord and Saviour. It is appropriate nowadays to question this: we now have such a proper respect for other faiths and practices that we can look back at the nineteenth-century missionaries and wonder if they were engaged in a kind of Christian imperialism, a takeover in the spiritual world that was equivalent to the colonial takeover of the British Empire.

Nevertheless, we should never forget the nobility and dedication of those who went out in the service of Christ. Charlotte Brontë described one of them in *Jane Eyre*. She finished the novel not (as one might expect) with the happy marriage of Jane and Rochester, but with St John Rivers, who went to India. Rivers has not been the most attractive character in the book, but he emerges at the end as a hero:

A more resolute, indefatigable pioneer never wrought amidst rocks and dangers. Firm, faithful, and devoted, full of energy, and zeal, and truth, he labours for his race. He clears their painful way to improvement; he hews down like a giant the prejudices of creed and caste that encumber it.

Rivers was one of thousands who went out to countries where their chances of survival for any length of time were slim. Those who went to West Africa, particularly, knew that they were going out with a life expectancy of one or two years at the most. One can only admire their steadfastness and courage, the courage of the noble army of martyrs. It is in this spirit that Ellerton's hymn was written.

It is a wonderful poetic achievement, for it moves from the human ordinariness of verse 1 to a vision of the globe, spinning in space, and then back to earth again at the end. In the process it takes us in a great leap from Genesis to Revelation. The first verse begins with 'The day thou gavest', which is from Genesis 1, in which God said 'Let there be light' and divided the light from the darkness. The last verse ends with all the creatures of the earth worshipping God, from Revelation 5:

> And every creature which is in heaven, and on the earth, and under the earth, and such as are in the sea, and all that are in them, heard I saying, Blessing, and honour, and glory, and power, be unto him that sitteth upon the throne, and unto the Lamb . . .'

It is a great vision of a missionary ideal. But if it is sung at funerals, so much the better. There is no point in being strict or possessive about its original meaning: hymns were made for people, and not people for hymns. Besides, it is very suitable for such occasions. 'The day thou gavest, Lord, is ended' could well be thought to refer, as it does in 'Abide with me', to the day of life, which is now over; and the hymn moves out from that to the great vision of Revelation 5. In the same way, funerals move us because they accept the fact of death, while presenting us with a hope of some kind of future life, a life which we can never really imagine but can just manage to speak of with the language of a visionary. So Ellerton's hymn beautifully begins with the ordinary, the here-and-now, and then opens out into a wonder which we can all find comforting. There is more to life than the material world: there are values of the spirit that are beyond the cognisance of 'earth's proud empires'. There is joy, and memory, and love; and, even as we mourn, the hope of heaven itself.

THE CHRISTIAN YEAR

O come, O come, Emmanuel

Latin, translated by
John Mason Neale (1818–66)

O come, O come, Emmanuel,
And ransom captive Israel,
That mourns in lonely exile here,
Until the Son of God appear:
  Rejoice! Rejoice! Emmanuel
  Shall come to thee, O Israel.

O come, thou Rod of Jesse, free
Thine own from Satan's tyranny;
From depths of hell thy people save,
And give them victory o'er the grave:
  Rejoice! Rejoice! Emmanuel
  Shall come to thee, O Israel.

O come, thou Dayspring, come and cheer
Our spirits by thine advent here;
Disperse the gloomy clouds of night,
And death's dark shadows put to flight:
  Rejoice! Rejoice! Emmanuel
  Shall come to thee, O Israel.

O come, thou Key of David, come,
And open wide our heavenly home;
Make safe the way that leads on high,
And close the path to misery:
  Rejoice! Rejoice! Emmanuel
  Shall come to thee, O Israel.

O come, O come, thou Lord of Might,
Who by thy tribes on Sinai's height,
In ancient times didst give the law
In cloud and majesty and awe:

Rejoice! Rejoice! Emmanuel
Shall come to thee, O Israel.

This hymn, perhaps more than any other, heralds the approach of Christmas. In the dark days at the end of November, these ancient words and music ring out to remind us that from this moment on there is, in the distance, the most touching of all Christian festivals. In December, in the gloomiest time of the year, and not far off the shortest day of the year, comes the gladdening of our hearts at the yearly remembrance of the birth of a baby in a stable. Soon we shall hear of the shepherds abiding in the fields, keeping watch over their flock by night, and of the wise men, led by a star to Bethlehem and the Christ child. Soon the first Christmas cards will be plopping through the letter box; soon we shall be thinking of the meeting of families, the company of friends, the annual kindnesses, the feasting and the laughter; soon we shall be thinking of carol services, and of Christmas music. And outside in the streets, all the shops, decorated for Christmas, would like to remind us that this is the time of year to buy presents for others and little luxuries for ourselves – or so they hope. For the other side of Christmas is the commercial one. In reaction to it, charities, quite rightly, ask for donations at Christmas. For many of us, Christmas is a chance to be a little bit more generous to those less well off than ourselves.

This is Christmas in the prosperous countries of the world, and for the fortunate ones in those countries. We should all give a thought to those who live in poverty, for whom Christmas is one more day in the unrelenting struggle against want and disease. And we should give a thought to the lonely, too: all the expectation of Christmas joy is hard if you have nobody to share it with. I suspect that, as Christmas approaches, we all have a confused jumble of feelings about ourselves and others: we may have those feelings all the time, but they emerge with particular sharpness at this time. We love the beauty of Christmas, and the enjoyment of it, but we also recognize and regret the unhappiness which others feel. It is as if, for a few days, the things that we delight in make life more difficult for them.

The season of Advent also produces mixed feelings. It is traditionally the beginning of the church year, the moment in which the pattern of thinking our way through the great events – Christmas, Easter, Pentecost – begins again. We look forward in hope to the Nativity, and every Sunday brings it closer: we remember the prophets, John the Baptist, the Virgin Mary herself. At the same time, it is a time for serious thought, for an appraisal of ourselves that is often hard and uncomfortable. Advent carol services traditionally end their readings with the passage from Matthew 25.31–46, which begins, 'When the Son of man shall come in his glory, and all the holy angels with him, then shall he sit upon the throne of his glory.' There follows the division of people into sheep and goats: into those who gave drink to the thirsty, room to the stranger, clothes to the naked, who visited the sick and the prisoners; and those who did none of these things. The fear of judgement is always with us in the season of Advent. It is spelt out in the Advent Collect, which thrills us every year as its words herald the coming of Christ. He comes in two ways: in great humility at Bethlehem, and in his glorious majesty as Judge of the living and the dead:

Almighty God, give us grace that we may cast away the works of darkness, and put upon us the armour of light, now in the time of this mortal life, in which thy Son Jesus Christ came to visit us in great humility; that in the last day, when he shall come in his glorious Majesty to judge both the quick and the dead, we may rise to the life immortal . . .

We are placed between hope and despair: Christ came to save us from sin, but he will also come as our judge. It is very right that we should feel penitent like this, after which Christmas comes as a comfort. Sometimes we sing Psalm 85 on Christmas morning: 'Mercy and truth are met together; righteousness and peace have kissed each other.' We feel the severity, but now it is tempered with mercy.

This hymn carries the same kind of multiple meaning. It is very old, perhaps going back to the eighth century. It must have echoed through the choirs of the monasteries in those far-off Decembers, year by year bringing hope at the darkest time of the year. I like to imagine the monks, by the flickering light of their candles, singing, '*Veni, veni, Emmanuel*', 'O come, O come, Emmanuel'. Come to us, who are the children of God, like the

Israelites in captivity in Babylon: 'ransom captive Israel / That mourns in lonely exile here'. The imagery is from the Old Testament, the sentiment from the New Testament: the Son of God will appear, and give his life a ransom for many (Mark 10.45, Matthew 20.28). So 'Rejoice': Emmanuel *shall* come to Israel.

In the monastic tradition, these Latin verses were called the 'O antiphons' or 'The Great Os'. They were sung at vespers during the seven days before Christmas Eve. When the monks reached the last of the great Os, they would know that only the vigil of Christmas Eve itself stood between them and the great feast of the Nativity. All that preparation of mind and of body (for some would have fasted, as in Lent) was about to give way to joy. Day by day they added a new verse. We do not usually sing them all, but some remain: the Rod of Jesse (from Isaiah 11.1 – 'And there shall come forth a rod out of the stem of Jesse', signifying Jesus's descent from the Old Testament patriarchs); the Dayspring (from Luke 1.78 – 'Through the tender mercy of our God; whereby the dayspring from on high hath visited us'); the Key of David (from Isaiah 22.22 and Revelation 3.7 – 'the key of the house of David ... so he shall open and none shall shut; and he shall shut and none shall open', here the key that will 'open wide our heavenly home' and 'shut the path to misery'); and the Lord of Might (the Lord who gave the tablets of the law to Moses on Mount Sinai, Exodus 19 and 20).

The last verse reminds us of the greatness of God. But the Old Testament figure who gave the law to Moses is also the Emmanuel of this hymn, the 'God with us' of Matthew 1.23: 'Behold, a virgin shall be with child, and shall bring forth a son, and they shall call his name Emmanuel, which being interpreted is, God with us.' The angel Gabriel, who speaks these words, was quoting from Isaiah 7.14. The prophecy has come to pass.

Each Christmas we record that prophecy and its fulfilment. Like the old monks, we sing of the coming of the Christ child in the days that lead up to the feast of the Nativity, and each year we feel its magic, as they must have done. For the righteousness of the Old Testament, which is so properly recalled in the final verse, is now tempered with mercy. As the third verse puts it, the gloomy clouds of night are dispersed, and the dark shadows of death are put to flight; which is why Advent carol services begin in darkness and end in light. The candles of those services symbolize the hope for humanity in a dark and sinful world: the hope that, however sinful we may be, we can be accepted by the God who came to earth as Christ Jesus. This belief makes a Christmas in the heart, as the American hymn writer Phillips Brooks put it:

> O holy child of Bethlehem,
>   Descend to us, we pray;
> Cast out our sin, and enter in,
>   Be born in us today.
> We hear the Christmas angels
>   The great glad tidings tell:
> O come to us, abide with us,
>   Our Lord Immanuel!

Once in royal David's city
Cecil Frances Alexander (1818–95)

Once in royal David's city
   Stood a lowly cattle-shed,
Where a mother laid her baby
   In a manger for his bed:
Mary was that mother mild,
Jesus Christ her little child.

He came down to earth from heaven
   Who is God and Lord of all
And his shelter was a stable,
   And his cradle was a stall;
With the poor and mean and lowly
Lived on earth our Saviour holy.

And through all his wondrous childhood
   He would honour and obey,
Love, and watch the lowly maiden
   In whose gentle arms he lay.
Christian children all must be
Mild, obedient, good as he.

For he is our childhood's pattern
   Day by day like us he grew,
He was little, weak and helpless,
   Tears and smiles like us he knew;
And he feeleth for our sadness,
And he shareth in our gladness.

And our eyes at last shall see him,
   Through his own redeeming love,
For that child so dear and gentle
   Is our Lord in heaven above;
And he leads his children on
To the place where he is gone.

Not in that poor lowly stable,
　With the oxen standing by,
We shall see him; but in heaven,
　Set at God's right hand on high;
When like stars his children crowned
All in white shall wait around.

This hymn is of course a favourite at Christmas-time. It has been used for many years as the processional hymn which begins the Festival of Nine Lessons and Carols from King's College, Cambridge, a service which has set the pattern for many others in churches and cathedrals all over the world. The singing of the first verse as a treble solo on a December afternoon makes a moment of singular enchantment: for many people this is the quintessential Christmas moment, a minute of perfect, measured sound cutting through the darkening silence. The commercialism and hassle of Christmas suddenly seem far away as the voice sings the well-known tune and begins to tell the familiar story once again.

The secret of this hymn is that it is a story for children. We all like to hear stories, children especially: they love to hear them again and again. This one begins with the suggestion of 'Once upon a time . . .' – 'Once in royal David's city . . .' – as though settling down to a fairy story with its traditional opening: 'Once upon a time, in David's city, there was a mother, who had a baby in a cattle shed . . . she was called Mary, and the baby's name was Jesus . . .' The language is suitable for children, but it will also serve for grown-ups; indeed grown-ups like it, because they often like good children's stories, and because at Christmas they can become for a moment like children again. This need not be childish: it can be innocent and healthy, as Dickens saw in *A Christmas Carol*: 'It is good to be children sometimes, and never better than at Christmas, when its mighty Founder was a child himself.'

Mrs Alexander's hymn is like this: not childish, but innocent. We all, old and young, listen to the story unfolding, almost as if we had never heard it before:

He came down to earth from heaven
　Who is God and Lord of all,
And his shelter was a stable,
　And his cradle was a stall . . .

In verse 3 this simplicity goes on, carrying the story through baby-hood and into childhood. As if in some Italian or Flemish paint-ing, the child lies in the mother's arms and looks at her; later he comes to honour and obey her. The moral comes in at this point: 'Christian children all must be / Mild, obedient, good as he.' For the first time the story is interrupted, with a gentle admonition, only to return to the narrative in the next verse – 'Day by day like us he grew' – as the hymn resumes its progress through the story. The words 'like us' are the important ones: they are there to remind children, and adults, of the full consequences of the birth of Jesus Christ in a stable at Bethlehem. In the words of Philippians 2, he 'made himself of no reputation, and took upon him the form of a servant, and was made in the likeness of men'. He humbled him-self, or (to put it in Charles Wesley's words) he 'emptied himself of all but love'.

In so doing he became fully human: he knew the total depend-ence of babyhood and the joys and sorrows of childhood, its tears and smiles. So he is able to feel human sadness and share in human gladness, because he has become a child himself, able to experience all the ups and downs of the day-to-day existence of a child, those emotional states which are experienced so intensely by children. The verse shows a vivid understanding of what it is like to be a child, as we reflect that if Jesus Christ was born in Bethlehem to poor parents, then he must have undergone all the passions that children have to live through – excitement, and joy, and anger, and tears. But, of course, he was also God, and this is addressed in the next verse, beginning, 'And our eyes at last shall see him'. It is there that the children are told that the child 'so dear and gentle' is also 'our Lord in heaven above'.

So the story has been told. Once upon a time, in the city of David called Bethlehem, there was a mother who gave birth to a baby in a stable and laid him in a manger; but that baby, who grew up as we all have to grow up, was actually our Lord himself, God almighty becoming a human being like the rest of us. But there is another side to that Lord God almighty, which one day we shall see: after his life, his death and resurrection and his ascension into heaven, then he will be found sitting at the right hand of the Father. It is to that glorious place that he leads his children: by the end of the hymn we have moved from the lowly cattle-shed, with the oxen standing by, to heaven, where the children stand around him like stars.

The contrast between the oxen on earth and the children in heaven is one of the many subtleties of this hymn. It seems to be a simple story, and it is written for young people, but in fact it is a profound meditation on the meaning of the Incarnation. It tells us that God was born in Christ so that we might go to heaven 'through his own redeeming love'. It moves from the earthly to the heavenly, from children on earth to children in heaven. Slowly and beautifully the pattern unfolds, from the tears and smiles of ordinary children to the crowned angels in white of the last line. Here the hymn draws on an ancient tradition: there were different 'orders' of angels, with the inferior ones acting as God's messengers, and the highest ones standing round God's throne and waiting upon him. Milton uses it in the sonnet on his blindness, in which 'thousands at his bidding speed' while the higher angels worship at the throne of God: 'They also serve who only stand and wait.'

These last two lines are like a picture from a Victorian illustrated book, in which angels have the innocent faces of children; or they could be a reminder that children often died young in the nineteenth century, and that in their innocence they become like angels in heaven; or the word 'children' could mean an element that exists in all of us, the childlike part of us that we hope will be one day ('at last') taken into heaven, and allowed to wear white, like those in Revelation 7.14, who 'came out of great tribulation, and have washed their robes, and made them white in the blood of the Lamb'. I suspect that all of these images are somehow present in the mind as the hymn soars into its final verse: it is as if the fairy story of the first verses had turned somehow into a magical vision of heaven with angels that are like children, whose purpose is to stand by the throne of God and serve him.

It is no good treating this hymn as if it were some theological treatise, or arguing about its reading of the psychology of children. Far too much criticism has been directed at 'Christian children all must be / Mild, obedient, good as he.' The hymn is beloved not for its message but for its magic. From the first moment of its 'Once upon a time' opening to the last vision of the angel-children like stars in heaven, it conducts us through a landscape of extraordinary beauty: first of a painting, and then of a glimpse of heaven. In this hymn there are no shepherds, no wise men, no angels singing in the sky, and only one glimpse of the oxen: it just concentrates on the child and his mother, and on the children to whom the story is told. And in so doing, it casts upon us its Christmas spell, a magic that enchants us, year after year.

Sing, my tongue, the glorious battle

Venantius Fortunatus (*c.*530–609), translated by Percy Dearmer (1867–1936) and John Mason Neale (1818–66)

———◗◆◖———

Sing, my tongue, the glorious battle,
  Sing the ending of the fray;
Now above the Cross, the trophy,
  Sound the loud triumphant lay:
Tell how Christ, the world's Redeemer,
  As a Victim won the day.

God in pity saw man fallen,
  Shamed and sunk in misery,
When he fell on death by tasting
  Fruit of the forbidden tree;
Then another tree was chosen
  Which the world from death should free.

Thus the scheme of our salvation
  Was of old in order laid,
That the manifold deceiver's
  Art by art might be outweighed,
And the lure the foe put forward
  Into means of healing made.

Therefore when the appointed fullness
  Of the holy time was come,
He was sent who maketh all things
  Forth from God's eternal home;

39

Thus he came to earth, incarnate,
    Offspring of a maiden's womb.

———————————

Thirty years among us dwelling,
    His appointed time fulfilled,
Born for this, he meets his Passion,
    For that this he freely willed,
On the Cross the Lamb is lifted
    Where his life-blood shall be spilled.

He endured the nails, the spitting,
    Vinegar, and spear, and reed;
From that holy Body broken
    Blood and water forth proceed:
Earth, and stars, and sky, and ocean
    By that flood from stain are freed.

Faithful Cross! Above all other,
    One and only noble tree!
None in foliage, none in blossom,
    None in fruit thy peer may be;
Sweetest wood and sweetest iron!
    Sweetest weight is hung on thee.

Bend thy boughs, O Tree of Glory!
    Thy relaxing sinews bend;
For awhile the ancient rigour
    That thy birth bestowed, suspend;
And the King of heavenly beauty
    On thy bosom gently tend!

Thou alone wast counted worthy
    This world's ransom to uphold;
For a shipwreck'd race preparing
    Harbour, like the Ark of old;
With the sacred Blood anointed
    From the smitten Lamb that rolled.

———————————

To the Trinity be glory
    Everlasting, as is meet;
Equal to the Father, equal
    To the Son, and Paraclete:

Trinal Unity, whose praises
All created things repeat. Amen.

St Radegunde, who lived from about 520 to 587, was of royal birth. In the manner of royal dynasties of the sixth century, she was married against her will to Clothar, king of the Franks. After he had murdered her brother, Radegunde escaped from the court and became a deaconess, living in poverty and founding a small community at Poitiers to care for the poor and sick. She went on to found a convent there. In the early Middle Ages, one of the desirable possessions of such a place was a relic of a saint, or some other holy object, which would encourage the visits of pilgrims; the monks at Conques, for example, stole the relics of Sainte Foy (St Faith) from the monks of Agen. Radegunde, using her aristocratic connections, obtained from the Byzantine Emperor Justin II a fragment of the true cross, which was brought to Poitiers in 569.

One of the members of the community at Poitiers was the poet Venantius Fortunatus, a friend of Radegunde, who later wrote her life. On the great occasion of the arrival of the piece of the true cross, he wrote two very grand hymns, *Vexilla Regis*, 'The royal banners forward go', and this one, *Pange, lingua, gloriosi proelium certaminis*, 'Sing, my tongue, the glorious battle'.

This is a great hymn because it is such a compressed statement of Christian doctrine, from the fall to the redemption. The story of the fall was created to explain our humanity: our original ideal state, and our separation from God in our present one, in which we distance ourselves from God by our selfishness, pride, envy, greed, and other sins. But the fall led to the redemption of the world, and so it is sometimes referred to as the *felix culpa*, or the fortunate fall. As Adam says in *Paradise Lost*, when he is told of the redemption that is to come:

Full of doubt I stand,
Whether I should repent me now of sin
By me done and occasioned, or rejoice
Much more, that much more good thereof shall spring,
To God more glory, more good will to men
From God, and over wrath grace shall abound.

(XII. 473–8)

Confronted with the fragment of the true cross, Venantius Fortunatus was inspired in the same way. He constructs a series of clever oppositions: to counter the tree of the Garden of Eden, God chose another tree, the cross; to thwart the bad art of the devil, God devised his own good art, the scheme of our salvation. He did so in the fullness of time, when the Creator became incarnate as the Redeemer.

In this hymn, a fragment of the cross, which is the symbol of that process, is *there*, before them as they sing: in its holy presence they feel closer to the miraculous event itself, the moment in which 'Christ, the world's Redeemer, / As a Victim won the day.' The paradox is clear: it is the victim who wins in this battle, because it is no ordinary battle. It is the victory of love over death, of goodness over hatred. And the relic itself is precious beyond measure: to possess it is somehow to feel that the event was true. The fragment of wood is authentic evidence: it can be touched or seen, and in touching it or seeing it faith is strengthened.

Later in the Middle Ages, of course, the provision of relics was grossly abused, and the whole practice got a bad name. Chaucer's Pardoner, in *The Canterbury Tales*, had a sack full of rags and bones which he pretended were holy. But back in 569 there seems no reason to doubt that a fragment was brought to Poitiers, and believed to be genuine. Venantius Fortunatus certainly thought so. It gave him the inspiration for the hymn, in which he celebrated the possession of the actual wood on which Christ had died.

Relics were, and are, important in themselves. But the vital distinction must be made between the worship of the relic itself and the worship of what the relic stands for. This is the burden of the hymn, which begins with 'the Cross, the trophy', but understands clearly that its subject is not the wood itself, but the sufferings and death of Jesus Christ, of which that wood was a participant and a witness. What that suffering and death involved is the subject of the second half of the hymn. In it, the Passion or suffering of Christ is portrayed: the nails, the spitting, the lifting up of the cross, the wound in the side. These all follow the narratives of the Gospels. But now comes the really imaginative and original part of the hymn: because the fragment of the true cross is before him, Fortunatus now addresses it, speaking to the inanimate wood as if it were alive and had feelings. The cross is reminded that it is a tree which is now greater than all other trees. It is no longer terrible, but precious:

> Sweetest wood and sweetest iron!
> Sweetest weight is hung on thee.

The pretence that the wood can feel is carried yet further in the next verse, which moves our minds back to the moment of Christ's suffering: 'Bend thy boughs, O Tree of Glory!' The cross, or tree, is urged to be gentle, to suspend its ancient rigour (the fact that it was born a piece of unbending and unyielding wood), and even to act as a comforting mother:

> And the King of heavenly beauty
> On thy bosom gently tend!

The cross is no longer an inanimate object: it has feelings, it is capable of love and comfort. It saves the human race from the shipwreck of sin, as Noah's ark did in the old legend. It holds up in its branches the ransom of the world, and from it rolls the blood of the Lamb that was slain. It speaks to us of many things, reminding us of the crucifixion itself but also of its many meanings: that this is the Lamb that was slain; that the Christ who hangs on the tree, covered in blood, is also the 'King of heavenly beauty'; that he gave his life a ransom for many; that on the cross he was a victim who was victorious.

The fragment of the true cross is thus a real piece of wood, but a piece of wood that provokes the imagination to dwell on the significance of the event of which it was a part. It is wood with a history, and that history makes it more precious than any other piece of wood in the world. We may imagine St Radegunde, the former queen who fled from her wicked husband and his corrupt court, enraptured at coming into possession of such a thing. The future of her convent was assured: it was renamed the Convent of the Holy Cross, and by the time of her death it had some 200 nuns. To them, as to her, the fragment would have been a living presence. It had touched the flesh of the Saviour, borne his body aloft, been stained with his blood. But as Venantius knew, it was not worshipped for its own sake, but for what it represented.

Protestants tend to see relics through the eyes of the reformers, who were anxious to stamp out the abuses of the later Middle

Ages. And in this post-Freudian age, relics can easily be seen as encouraging superstition and dubious practices. But there is also something mysterious and wonderful about a physical object which has survived from another age and another event – St Cuthbert's coffin, Guy Fawkes's lantern, Mary Queen of Scots' keys. We can, of course, be sceptical, or pretend that these things mean nothing to us. But that would be a pity. As Samuel Johnson said when visiting Iona,

> Whatever withdraws us from the power of our senses; whatever makes the past, the distant, or the future predominate over the present, advances us in the dignity of thinking beings . . . That man is little to be envied whose patriotism would not gain force upon the plain of Marathon, or whose piety would not grow warmer among the ruins of Iona.

And whether we believe in relics or not, we can surely understand the excitement which the nuns at Poitiers must have felt in the year 569, and respect it. It allowed Fortunatus to write one of the great hymns of the early Church, because he allowed his imagination to dwell on the cross, not as a relic, but as an emblem of salvation.

When I survey the wondrous cross
Isaac Watts (1674–1748)

When I survey the wondrous cross,
   On which the Prince of Glory died,
My richest gain I count but loss,
   And pour contempt on all my pride.

Forbid it, Lord, that I should boast
   Save in the death of Christ my God;
All the vain things that charm me most,
   I sacrifice them to his blood.

See from his head, his hands, his feet,
   Sorrow and love flow mingled down;
Did e'er such love and sorrow meet,
   Or thorns compose so rich a crown?

His dying crimson, like a robe,
   Spreads o'er his body on the tree;
Then am I dead to all the globe,
   And all the globe is dead to me.

Were the whole realm of nature mine,
   That were a present far too small;
Love so amazing, so divine,
   Demands my soul, my life, my all.

This is the greatest English hymn on the Passion of Christ written since the Reformation. The Passion, or suffering, of Christ, was a common subject of early and medieval hymns and poems, from the Anglo-Saxon 'The Dream of the Rood' onwards; and this tradition was carried on by George Herbert in his poem 'The Sacrifice'. But no other hymn written in English has described the suffering of Christ with such dignity and restraint, while at the same time allowing us to feel the power of the moment so deeply.

It is almost as if the holding back of emotion in the words produces an increase of feeling in the reader or singer. Those carefully paced lines require us quietly and reverently to approach the great mystery of the suffering Christ, and to ponder its meaning slowly.

For the hymn is not just about the crucifixion. It is about our response to that event. It is not based on one of the Gospel accounts of the death of Jesus Christ, but upon a verse from St Paul's Epistle to the Galatians (6.14): 'But God forbid that I should glory, save in the cross of our Lord Jesus Christ, by whom the world is crucified unto me, and I unto the world.' The verse is about how we should behave in the face of such a tremendous event as God, in Christ, hanging on a cross for us. So the hymn begins with 'I': 'When I survey', as though the speaker is someone looking on, quietly watching. And yet he also knows that this is a 'wondrous cross', something wonderful, a cross on which a prince of glory died – not any prince of glory, but *the* Prince of Glory: the Son of God who (as St Paul reminds us in Philippians 2) 'humbled himself, and became obedient unto death, even the death of the cross'. It is a little like the experience of looking at an Italian painting of the crucifixion: you are invited to stand in front of it, look at it, and allow it to engage with your emotions. Yet you are conscious that you are not just the spectator, standing in front of the picture: you are also a human being, and you allow it to work its way through to your inmost self, through the eyes to the mind and soul.

And how do that mind and soul respond? That is the question that this hymn so wonderfully addresses. The first verse tells us that, in the face of such an extraordinary event as the crucifixion of the Prince of Glory, all human values are turned upside down:

> My richest gain I count but loss,
> And pour contempt on all my pride.

Pride, self-esteem, achievement: all these things disappear in the contemplation of the figure on the cross; and the second verse, which is very close to the verse from Galatians, drives this home. There is nothing to boast of in any human virtue: 'God forbid that I should glory, save in the cross of our Lord Jesus Christ . . .' Before the blood of the crucified Christ, all the vain things of life are willingly sacrificed.

These first two verses revise all our normal ways of looking at things. Gain becomes loss, pride becomes contemptible, the charms of the world are sacrificed. We now discover why. What is it that flows from the Prince of Glory on the tree? Blood, of course. But what is that blood composed of? Corpuscles, white cells, plasma, yes. But a person's 'blood' is more than this. It is a measure of character. We speak of someone being 'hot-blooded' or 'cold-blooded', or courageous – 'his blood was up'. Here, in a brilliant transformation, the blood that comes from the bleeding Christ is 'sorrow and love', 'love and sorrow'. The repetition takes us deeper and deeper into the dual nature of the blood, and into the character of Christ himself. He is made up of sorrow, which is an echo of Lamentations 1.12: 'Is it nothing to you, all ye that pass by? behold, and see if there be any sorrow like unto my sorrow . . .'

But he is also made up of love, the love that died on the cross for human sin. The two things meet, cross over, sorrow and love – love and sorrow – and then meet again. The blood flows from the wounds made by the thorns, but those thorns compose a crown that is richer than any earthly crown; just as the love and sorrow are the purest elements of the divine blood. That blood, the 'dying crimson', gradually spreads over his body. Now we are in the present tense: we have been since the beginning of verse 3. We can see that in singing this hymn we have become participants in the scene, watchers at the crucifixion itself, seeing the blood spreading over the body in a kind of red robe. It is startlingly vivid and it is overwhelming. As the spectator watches, the world becomes nothing:

> Then am I dead to all the globe,
> And all the globe is dead to me.

Once again the words cross over: they show the normal interaction between the self and the outside world (world–self–self–world), and turn it to nothing. We all perceive the world around us, and have a perpetual interaction with it – the internal interprets the external, the external influences the internal. This is what happens all the time in normal circumstances. But now, in the face of this amazing event, the process goes dead. Or, as St Paul put it, the cross of our Lord Jesus Christ is the single important thing in history.

The dying Christ is the one 'by whom the world is crucified unto me, and I unto the world'.

In these two verses, the singer becomes a participant at the crucifixion itself. Watts allows us to come closer and exclaim – 'See from his head, his hands, his feet'. In the last verse, the reader or singer reflects. I like to think of him, on that far-off Friday afternoon, walking off the scene. He goes home after seeing a man, all made of sorrow and love, crucified between two thieves. As he goes, he meditates on what he has seen. His thoughts make up the most demanding verse in English hymnody. If he had the whole of nature at his disposal, that would be too small a present; such love requires the dedication of himself – 'my soul, my life, my all'. Indeed, it is more than dedication. It is a total self-surrender, and one that comes naturally after what has gone before.

Every Passion-tide, when we sing this hymn, it bears down upon us with a weight of expectation. The last verb in the hymn is 'demands'. But that expectation, that demand, is justified by the extraordinary way in which Watts unobtrusively reminds us of the meaning of what happened. On a cross was the Prince of Glory, Christ my God, suffering and shedding blood, the blood of sorrow but also the blood of love. The consolation is tremendous, as well as the demand. For what it shows is something 'so amazing, so divine'. And if the last verb of the hymn is 'demands', the last subject of that verb is 'Love'.

Holy, Holy, Holy!
Lord God Almighty
Reginald Heber (1783–1826)

Holy, Holy, Holy! Lord God Almighty!
  Early in the morning our song shall rise to thee;
Holy, Holy, Holy! merciful and mighty!
  God in three Persons, blessed Trinity!

Holy, Holy, Holy! all the saints adore thee,
  Casting down their golden crowns around the glassy sea;
Cherubim and Seraphim falling down before thee,
  Which wert, and art, and evermore shall be.

Holy, Holy, Holy! though the darkness hide thee,
  Though the eye of sinful man thy glory may not see,
Only thou art holy, there is none beside thee
  Perfect in power, in love, and purity.

Holy, Holy, Holy! Lord God Almighty!
  All thy works shall praise thy name, in earth and sky and sea;
Holy, Holy, Holy! merciful and mighty!
  God in three Persons, blessed Trinity!

Reginald Heber, poet, academic and clergyman, became Bishop of Calcutta in 1823. Calcutta was a huge diocese, with responsibilities over a wide area, and Heber died suddenly after three years in the post, possibly as the result of overwork in a hot climate. He is one of the heroes of the 'mission field' of the nineteenth century, for which he wrote 'From Greenland's icy mountains'. This hymn is about the mysterious and wonderful.

It is for Trinity Sunday. It is based on the threefold *Sanctus*, the 'Holy, holy, holy', taken originally from Isaiah 6.3 and used in the service of Holy Communion at the moment of giving thanks

49

following the 'comfortable words' of the Absolution. Its threefold repetition alludes to the three-personed Trinity itself – Father, Son and Holy Ghost – and it is a suitable expression of awe and wonder at the contemplation of the great mystery of the God-head. Indeed, 'mystery' is the right word to use. Originally the word meant 'a religious truth known only from divine revelation . . . usually a doctrine of the faith involving difficulties which human reason is incapable of solving' (*Oxford English Dictionary*). Later it was used to mean 'something hidden'. The Holy Trinity is certainly something hidden from us, as another hymn says:

> Immortal, invisible, God only wise,
> In light inaccessible, hid from our eyes . . .

It is said that in some monasteries in the Middle Ages there was a rule that a sermon should be preached on every Sunday of the year except for Trinity Sunday, when the subject was thought to be too difficult. Yet the concept of the triune God has always been thought necessary to try to express something of the wonder and glory of the divine.

All worshippers feel the need to adore the God who is the centre of the universe and the ground of all being, and the three-fold nature of the Holy Trinity corresponds to that human need: to adore the God who created the world and who is the source of all life; the Son of God, who died and rose again to conquer death; and the Holy Spirit, that power which comes from God and which works within us. Each of these elements is saluted by its 'Holy', and what this hymn does is to allow full expression to these complex ideas of what we think of as God. And as we think of God, so our souls and bodies are caught up in a rapture of contemplation: we adore ideal beauty, truth, goodness, selfless love, and individual power. We move from our ordinary everyday selves into a contemplation of the sublime. We move from earth to heaven.

This corresponds to a very deep impulse in all of us to admire perfection and to seek after it. We can all have glimpses of this in the loveliness of the world, and the beauty of human character. We can be moved to tears by music, or poetry, or the contempla-tion of a beautiful picture, or the grace of a dancer. At such mo-ments, we feel greater and better than we usually do: our normal selfhood is raised to a higher level as we contemplate a moment of perfection. This hymn gives words to the most glorious encounter of all, between the human and the divine.

The first verse, for example, begins with the majestic 'Holy, Holy, Holy! Lord God Almighty!', which brings us face to face with a power immeasurably greater than ourselves. Yet in line 2 we are reminded of who we are, human beings in church: 'Early in the morning our song shall rise to thee.' This echoes Psalm 63.1: 'O God, thou art my God: early will I seek thee'; it suggests a morning service, either Holy Communion or Morning Prayer. There we pray to God, but we have to have some idea of what God is like, so the third line reminds us of his chief attributes, power and love: he is God who is 'merciful and mighty'. We know that he is all-powerful; we live through the promise of his mercy.

But how can we imagine God? The next verse does so by painting a picture. Around God are the 24 elders, clothed in white, casting down their crowns before the throne, which has before it a sea of glass like crystal. It is taken from Revelation 4, with cherubim and seraphim added. It is the kind of scene which Italian painters loved to convey, a moment of magnificence in which all their joy in light and colour and form was employed in the presentation of glory (there is just such a picture, brilliantly placed, at the top of the stairway in the Sainsbury Wing of the National Gallery in London). In the face of such perfection we are conscious that we are ordinary mortals, who are subject to time and all the other conditions of human life. We are born, grow up, become old, and die. Line 4 of this second verse reminds us that God is beyond all this. God was, and is, and ever shall be. In God tenses do not exist: past, present and future are all made irrelevant. It is we who change: as Psalm 90 puts it, we spend our years as a tale that is told, and the days of our years are threescore and ten, but 'even from everlasting to everlasting, thou art God'. We are the human beings who sang in the early morning service, but the God to whom we sang is the God who existed before the mountains were brought forth, and who will be there for ever and ever.

But as verse 3 makes clear, God is hidden. The other meaning of 'mystery' finds its expression. God is in a profound and mysterious darkness, as he was even hidden from Moses (Exodus 20.21) and when 'he made darkness his secret place' (Psalm 18.11).

So although we can share the radiant vision of Revelation 4, and enjoy its representation in pictorial art, there is ultimately a holiness and inaccessibility which is beyond all our imaginings. We are human and sinful – 'Though the eye of sinful man thy glory may not see' – while God is unique – 'There is none beside thee' – and perfect – 'Perfect in power, in love, and purity'.

As so often in this hymn the poet works in threes, the words answering the threefold nature of God and echoing 'Holy, holy, holy': past, present, future; power, love, purity; and now, in the final verse, earth and sky and sea. This is the only line in the last verse that makes it different from the first verse, and it does so for a purpose. It takes us back to Revelation, this time to chapter 5:

> And every creature which is in heaven, and on the earth, and under
> the earth, and such as are in the sea, and all that are in them, heard
> I saying, 'Blessing, and honour, and glory, and power, be unto him
> that sitteth upon the throne, and unto the Lamb for ever and ever.'

The vision is a glorious one: everything in the hymn has led up to this point. We have encountered God as merciful, as mighty, as perfect, as unique, as hidden and mysterious, known to us only as God in three persons, as the blessed Trinity. All our attempts to describe him fall short of the glory of God – Father, Son and Holy Spirit. They do so because we are human and sinful; but we can aspire towards that glory, and in that aspiration we can become, for a moment, transformed by the power of our own vision. We become, for a moment, greater than ourselves.

THE COMMUNION
OF SAINTS

For all the saints who from their labours rest

William Walsham How (1823–97)

For all the saints who from their labours rest,
Who thee by faith before the world confessed,
Thy name, O Jesu, be for ever blest:
    Alleluia!

Thou wast their rock, their fortress, and their might;
Thou, Lord, their captain in the well-fought fight;
Thou in the darkness drear their one true light:
    Alleluia!

O may thy soldiers, faithful, true and bold,
Fight as the saints who nobly fought of old,
And win, with them, the victor's crown of gold:
    Alleluia!

O blest communion, fellowship divine!
We feebly struggle, they in glory shine;
Yet all are one in thee, for all are thine:
    Alleluia!

And when the strife is fierce, the warfare long,
Steals on the ear the distant triumph song,
And hearts are brave again, and arms are strong:
    Alleluia!

The golden evening brightens in the west;
Soon, soon to faithful warriors cometh rest;
Sweet is the calm of paradise the blest:
    Alleluia!

But lo, there breaks a yet more glorious day:
The saints triumphant rise in bright array;

The King of Glory passes on his way:
Alleluia!

From earth's wide bounds, from ocean's farthest coast,
Through gates of pearl streams in the countless host,
Singing to Father, Son, and Holy Ghost:
Alleluia!

This is a hymn of great splendour. It is suitable for a great occasion in a large church or a cathedral, when it can be used as a long processional hymn. Part of its effect must be owing to the tune Sine Nomine (meaning 'without a name'), which was written for it by Ralph Vaughan Williams: that tune carries the long lines with great force and energy, building up to the repeated 'Alleluia' at the end of each verse. And the verses succeed each other like waves breaking on the shore (this effect must have been even more remarkable in its original form, when it had 11 verses).

It is a hymn for All Saints' Day, 1 November, and one suggestion about the name of the tune is that it refers to saints who are forgotten, who have no name. They belong in the glorious company of those who lived on earth, and fought the good fight, and have now entered into their reward in heaven. The first two verses bless God for them, remembering how God in Jesus Christ was their rock and their strength; then the hymn moves into the present tense, with a reminder that the fight is still going on and that we are the soldiers who have to take part in it. The struggle between the forces of good and of evil is an idea which has great power: it is the central concept in Tolkien's *The Lord of the Rings*, in which the power of the evil Sauron will be complete if he can gain possession of the most powerful ring of all. Frodo and Sam undertake the dangerous quest to destroy the ring, and finally succeed in doing so, at the same time as the forces of good are struggling against the forces of evil.

This hymn has the same fascination as Tolkien's quest story. It tells of the victorious saints, and it recognizes the struggling saints of today. These are the soldiers of Christ, who have been celebrated in hymns again and again – 'Soldiers of Christ, arise'; 'Onward, Christian soldiers'. The original of this is the command of St Paul to Timothy in his first letter, 'Fight the good fight of faith' (1 Timothy 6.12), and the soldierly admonition in the second letter, 'Endure hardness, as a good soldier of Jesus Christ' (2 Timothy 2.3). In this second letter St Paul makes much of endurance and hardship, as elements of the soldier's life. It was written from Rome, when he was brought before the Emperor Nero for the second time; he was in great danger. But he rejoices, near the end of the second letter: 'I have fought a good fight, I have finished my course, I have kept the faith: Henceforth there is laid up for me a crown of righteousness, which the Lord, the righteous judge, shall give me at that day.'

It is possible to see this spirit as operating throughout the hymn. Life is a battlefield, and we are soldiers in it daily. Paul thought, rightly, that he had acquitted himself well, like a gallant hero in battle. He had kept the faith. In the hymn we pray that we, Christ's soldiers, may be like the saints, 'and win, with them, the victor's crown of gold'. We are not like them, for they have attained to glory, while we struggle on; yet through the struggle there is the hope that victory will one day come to us as it did to them. At the moment that the strife is fierce and the warfare long, there comes a bugle-call of hope, so that 'hearts are brave again, and arms are strong'. And then comes the evening, the golden evening, when the faithful warriors can have rest from the long day of battle.

The hymn vividly takes up the idea of a long day's fighting, and the reward for those who hold out to the end. But it also affirms the continuity of the tradition of Christian soldiership, the way in which, as we fight on, feebly struggling through our own time on this earth, we are following in the footsteps of those who have gone before. The original title of the hymn was 'Saints'-Day hymn. "A Cloud of Witnesses" – Heb. 12.1.' That quotation from Hebrews follows a long chapter which reminds the reader of the great heroes of old – Abraham, Isaac, Jacob, Abraham, Moses; and all the others, of whom (as the author tells us) 'the time would fail me to tell' – Gideon, and Barak, and Samson, and Jephtha, and David, and Samuel, and the prophets. And then he says:

> Wherefore seeing we also are compassed about with so great a cloud of witnesses, let us lay aside every weight, and the sin which doth so easily beset us, and let us run with patience the race that is set before us, Looking unto Jesus, the author and finisher of our faith; who for the joy that was set before him endured the cross, despising the shame, and is set down at the right hand of the throne of God.

Jesus is the greatest of all; but between Jesus and ourselves are all the other saints, who form the great cloud of witnesses. They have 'witnessed' to their faith: we could also say that, having attained their glory, they are 'witnesses' now of our struggle against sin and wickedness on the earth.

These are 'the saints triumphant' of the last two verses. They pass before us like a victorious army, or like soldiers on parade while 'The King of Glory passes on his way'. And then, like some passing-out parade, they march into heaven through the gates of pearl, singing to the Holy Trinity – Father, Son and Holy Ghost – 'Alleluia! Alleluia!' It is a magnificent and awe-inspiring vision, which brings the hymn to an end in glory. It is inspirational, and rightly so: all soldiers need to be warned that their life will be hard, but they also need to be inspired. This is why young recruits are taught regimental history, and why the flags and cap-badges of regiments carry the record of campaigns and battles. They will need all the endurance and courage they can muster, but they can take their place as part of a long and glorious history. And here, the hymn ends in a vision of the saints in glory that should make us all wish to follow in their footsteps, however feebly we struggle to do so: the communion of saints means that we should feel something wonderful, the communication with the glorious dead. As we think of the beliefs that bind us to them, one great fellowship of heaven and earth, we are, for a moment, cheered and inspired. Our morale is raised: we straighten our spiritual backs, hold our heads up, and march out to battle. As we look back at the lives of 'all the saints', we marvel at them, and try to emulate them. We may never live up to those aims and hopes, but even in trying to do so we do well: we are inspired to play our part in the coming of the kingdom of God, and we catch a glimpse of a finer and nobler world.

HOLY COMMUNION

Alleluia, sing to Jesus
William Chatterton Dix (1837–98)

Alleluia, sing to Jesus,
  His the sceptre, his the throne;
Alleluia, his the triumph,
  His the victory alone;
Hark, the songs of peaceful Sion
  Thunder like a mighty flood;
Jesus, out of every nation
  Hath redeemed us by his blood.

Alleluia, not as orphans
  Are we left in sorrow now;
Alleluia, he is near us,
  Faith believes, nor questions how;
Though the cloud from sight received him,
  When the forty days were o'er,
Shall our hearts forget his promise,
  'I am with you evermore'?

Alleluia, bread of angels,
  Thou on earth our food, our stay;
Alleluia, here the sinful
  Flee to thee from day to day;
Intercessor, friend of sinners,
  Earth's redeemer, plead for me,
Where the songs of all the sinless
  Sweep across the crystal sea.

Alleluia, King eternal,
  Thee the Lord of lords we own;
Alleluia, born of Mary,
  Earth thy footstool, heaven thy throne:
Thou within the veil has entered,
  Robed in flesh, our great High Priest;

Thou on earth both priest and victim
In the Eucharistic Feast.

This is a hymn by the Bristol poet William Chatterton Dix, published in his *Altar Songs: Verses on the Holy Eucharist* in 1867. I suspect that Dix's parents hoped that he would be a poet, for the 'Chatterton' is a reminder of the young Thomas Chatterton, who lived in Bristol a century earlier and wrote very fine mock-medieval poetry (the 'William' may have been after Shakespeare too). Dix lived up to his parents' expectations, publishing several volumes of religious poetry. This hymn is a splendid and forceful hymn, with a grand opening which gradually turns into a reflect-ive and prayerful exploration of the nature of Christ as redeemer. Indeed, the title of the hymn was 'Redemption by the Precious Blood', which makes it sound like a hymn from the Evangelical Revival of the eighteenth century; but Dix was a high churchman, and it combines that emphasis on the saving blood of Christ with the reminder of his sacrifice in the Holy Communion:

Almighty God, our heavenly Father, who of thy tender mercy didst give thine only Son Jesus Christ to suffer death upon the cross for our redemption; who made there (by his one oblation of himself once offered) a full, perfect, and sufficient sacrifice, oblation, and satisfaction, for the sins of the whole world . . .

If we think of the hymn as a versification of this sublime moment, we can see that it takes the idea and expands it, makes it new. The first verse does not dwell on the suffering of Christ, but on its triumphant outcome. The singer is invited to contemplate the great mystery and wonder of redemption in lines that deliberately emphasize the grandeur of the risen and ascended Lord: 'His the sceptre, his the throne'. His is the triumph and the victory, and to him are sung the songs of Sion, which are peaceful but also magnificent in their sound, thundering like a mighty river or a waterfall. Then, and only then, do we learn the reason for this grand opening: 'Jesus, out of every nation / Hath redeemed us by his blood.'

Dix is quoting here from Revelation 5.9: 'For thou wast slain, and hast redeemed us to God by thy blood out of every kindred, and tongue, and people, and nation.' It is a reminder that the triumph was hard-earned: but this is an after-Easter hymn, celebrating the risen and ascended Christ. This is made clear in verse 2, which reminds us that the Jesus who sits on the throne at the right hand of the Father in glory is the Jesus who lived among his disciples, who made them promises, and who sent the Holy Spirit as a comforter when he left the earth. The same verse alludes to his departure – 'though the cloud from sight received him, / when the forty days were o'er' – but assures us that we are not like children who have lost their parents, because he is with us, fulfilling his promise, 'Lo, I am with you alway, even unto the end of the world' (Matthew 28.20).

Dix is a master at blending different references from the Bible into one whole: there are references in this verse to the ascension itself, from Acts 1, and to the three chapters in St John's Gospel (14—16) in which Jesus comforts his disciples, telling them that he will be leaving them to go to the Father and promising them the gift of the Holy Ghost. The hymn then applies these wonders to the human condition: Christ, who sustains the very angels in heaven ('bread of angels') is our food ('I am the bread of life') on earth, the one to whom the sinful turn for forgiveness, day by day. And then suddenly the hymn becomes a prayer: 'Intercessor, friend of sinners, / Earth's redeemer, plead for me'. It is a wonderful moment; after all the grandeur, all the celebration, all the recapitulation of the life of Jesus, comes this cry for help: in your great majesty, after all that you have done for mankind, after your death, resurrection and ascension, now that you are in your glory, and across the crystal sea sweep the songs of all the sinless, plead for *me*. Remember your role as friend of sinners and redeemer of the earth, and plead for this little insignificant human being, this 'me', worshipper, sinner, ordinary human being.

The hymn is about the complex relationships that exist between us and God. It is the human role to worship and celebrate, to sing 'Alleluia' in every verse; but it is also a human duty to acknowledge the enormous distance between God in his glory and ourselves as sinners. There is perfection in heaven, and imperfection on earth: as Robert Browning wrote in 'Abt Vogler', 'On the earth the broken arcs; in the heaven a perfect round.' It is this great gap which Dix bridges in the final verse. Jesus is the 'King eternal' who was himself incarnate, 'born of Mary', and who is therefore both human and divine, priest and victim.

The solution to the problem of the purity of God and the sin of humanity is found in the doctrine of Christ as the great High Priest, which Dix beautifully deploys in the final verse. It comes from Hebrews 4—10, which refers back to Old Testament practices and the function of the High Priest, which was to offer sacrifices and burnt offerings in the holy place. This has been superseded, says the author of the Epistle, by Christ as a new kind of High Priest, 'who is set on the right hand of the throne of the Majesty in the heavens' (8.1). He does not need to offer up daily sacrifices as the old priests did, 'for this he did once, when he offered up himself' (7.27). So sinners can have 'boldness to enter into the holiest by the blood of Jesus, By a new and living way, which he hath consecrated for us, through the veil, that is to say, his flesh' and we have 'an high priest over the house of God' (10.19–21).

Jesus is now the High Priest, as the Epistle says. In Dix's hymn he has become human for us, robed in human flesh which is the 'veil' over his true Godhead; and in that humanity he becomes the 'victim', the Jesus whose death on the cross is at the centre of the Holy Communion. But because he is also, as in Hebrews, our great High Priest, he is both priest *and* victim: he is the Son of God, in his post-ascension glory, and also the God-Man who died for our sins and whose flesh we eat and whose blood we drink in remembrance of his suffering. As George Herbert wrote in his poem 'The Agonie':

> Love is that liquor sweet and most divine,
> Which my God feels as blood; but I, as wine.

Herbert and Dix both perform a poetic miracle, finding language to express the great mystery that lies at the heart of the Eucharist.

The King of love my Shepherd is
Henry Williams Baker (1821–77)

————◆————

The King of love my Shepherd is,
  Whose goodness faileth never;
I nothing lack if I am his
  And he is mine for ever.

Where streams of living water flow
  My ransomed soul he leadeth,
And, where the verdant pastures grow,
  With food celestial feedeth.

Perverse and foolish oft I strayed,
  But yet in love he sought me,
And on his shoulder gently laid,
  And home, rejoicing, brought me.

In death's dark vale I fear no ill
  With thee, dear Lord, beside me;
Thy rod and staff my comfort still,
  Thy cross before to guide me.

Thou spread'st a table in my sight;
  Thy unction grace bestoweth;
And oh, what transport of delight
  From thy pure chalice floweth!

And so through all the length of days
  Thy goodness faileth never:
Good Shepherd, may I sing thy praise
  Within thy house for ever.

This is one of the many metrical versions of Psalm 23. That psalm is perhaps the best loved of all the psalms for its comfort to the distressed and its vision of tranquillity and peace:

The Lord is my shepherd; I shall not want.
He maketh me to lie down in green pastures: he leadeth me
beside the still waters.
He restoreth my soul: he leadeth me in the paths of righteousness
for his name's sake.

This version is by Sir Henry Williams Baker, who was vicar of the
village of Monkland in Herefordshire, and the principal editor of
Hymns Ancient and Modern. He was brave to take on yet another
paraphrase of this beloved psalm, because he had before him the
well-known versions by George Herbert and Joseph Addison,
'The God of love my shepherd is' and 'The Lord my pasture shall
prepare', not to mention the Scottish 'The Lord's my shepherd,
I'll not want'. He succeeded triumphantly, helped by the beautiful
tune, Dominus Regit Me, by John Bacchus Dykes. One element of
the success comes from the shape of the verses, with the graceful
double rhyme at the end of lines 2 and 4 of each verse. That double
rhyme gives the reader or singer a very satisfying moment, as the
end of the verse picks up on the sound that has been hanging in
the air from line 2: 'leadeth / feedeth' . . . 'sought me / brought
me' . . . 'beside me / guide me'. The regular structure and the fluid
movement of the verses make the hymn seem predictable (metri-
cally) and comforting, which is as it should be.

Indeed, the other feature of this version of the psalm is its
stress on comfort and safety. The actual word 'comfort' appears
in verse 4 – 'Thy rod and staff my comfort still' – and in the psalm
itself: but here the whole hymn subtly emphasizes the perpetual
care and love of God. He is the shepherd in line 1, but he is also
'the King of love', and that love is shown in his tender care. He is
the one 'whose goodness faileth never' in line 2, and that promise
is taken up and repeated at the very end. The first two verses follow the psalm quite closely in this, but the third verse adds something to the idea of the sheep and the shepherd: 'Perverse and
foolish oft I strayed'. The tenderness of this verse is conveyed in
the picture of the shepherd going out after the lost sheep, placing
it on his shoulder, and bringing it home. It comes from the parable of the lost sheep in Luke 15.4–7, but also from the General
Confession which Baker would have recited every day as a priest
of the Church of England: 'Almighty and most merciful Father;
We have erred, and strayed from thy ways like lost sheep.'

In the General Confession the genuine sorrow at the evil we have done and at the good we have not done is balanced by the joy at knowing that God is the good shepherd, waiting and searching for his strayed sheep. As Charles Wesley put it, in words of crystalline simplicity, 'This man receiveth sinners still.' As we sing 'Perverse and foolish oft I strayed', we pick up the echo of the General Confession, but also the perpetual presence of forgiving love: 'oft I strayed . . . but yet in love he sought me.' Then the shepherd takes the lost sheep and carries it home, to the place where it should be. But he does so 'gently'; that word carries so much meaning about the nature of divine love that it is hard to overestimate its importance here. God's love in this hymn is the love of a caring shepherd, one who is gentle with his lost sheep and who feels tenderly towards them.

John Ellerton (who wrote 'The day thou gavest, Lord, is ended'), said that Baker spoke the words of this verse just before he died. If this is true, and there seems no reason to doubt it, it is a reminder of how that verse can reach out into the darkest places and bring comfort and hope. We have to imagine Baker, the country clergyman, ending his life in the assurance of the tender mercy of God and in the belief that although he had often strayed he was now finally being 'brought home'. For the psalm goes on to address the ultimate place of fear, the valley of the shadow of death, bringing to it the comfort of the presence of God as guide; for God has been there too, in the death of Jesus Christ upon the cross. In Baker's hymn, the rod and staff are 'my comfort still' but, he adds, 'Thy cross before to guide me'.

It is at this point that we notice the way in which the psalm has been transformed. Baker is writing a New Testament version of an Old Testament psalm, and the shepherd is now the Saviour who came to give his life as a ransom for many (Matthew 20.28). The idea is found in verse 2, where the shepherd leads his sheep to 'streams of living water' (from John 4) and the soul is 'my ransomed soul'. So we follow the New Testament in celebrating Jesus as the good shepherd: 'I am the good shepherd: the good shepherd giveth his life for the sheep' (John 10.11). The great commemoration of this is in the Holy Communion, in which we eat the bread and drink of the cup 'in remembrance of his death and passion'; and I like to imagine Baker, in his parish church,

Sunday by Sunday, saying those words and relating them to the words of Psalm 23, which are now given a new and more wonderful meaning: 'Thou preparest a table before me in the presence of mine enemies: thou anointest my head with oil; my cup runneth over.' Now the table is spread again, and the unction (anointing) bestows grace, and a 'transport of delight' flows from the chalice. Baker is describing the Eucharist as an experience of the love of the Saviour. 'Unction' is not only the actual use of holy oil itself but a symbol of all that the Eucharist does, bathing the forehead of the believer in the forgiving love of the Saviour, whose blood is drunk from the pure chalice.

By a parish priest such as Baker, the service of Holy Communion is celebrated daily, year after year, season after season. And so he brings us back to where we began, with a reminder that 'thy goodness faileth never'. But the celebration of the Eucharist is, as the Book of Common Prayer reminds us, 'a perpetual memory of that his precious death, until his coming again'. It is for this reason that the last verse begins, 'And so through all the length of days / Thy goodness faileth never.' The twenty-third psalm has become a great hymn of thankfulness and praise for the love of God in Christ Jesus and the daily celebration of that love in the Eucharist. And that happiness will, he hopes, be continued after death: 'Good Shepherd, may I sing thy praise / Within thy house for ever.'

The hymn places the emphasis on the tender and loving purposes of God, and on the gentleness of his forgiving love. That stress on comfort may not please those who feel that the Christian life should be always strenuous: indeed, an American writer, Love Maria Willis, wrote a kind of counter-text to Psalm 23 in a hymn beginning 'Father, hear the prayer we offer':

> Not for ever in green pastures
>   Do we ask our way to be;
> But the steep and rugged pathway
>   May we tread rejoicingly.
>
> Not for ever by still waters
>   Would we idly rest and stay . . .

Willis makes a point, and suits another mood, and introduces another kind of strenuous Christianity. But Baker's hymn speaks to something deep within us all: the consciousness of erring and straying like lost sheep; the trust in the tender love of one who described himself as the good shepherd; and the hope of being, in the end, 'brought home'.

GOD: FATHER, SON
AND HOLY SPIRIT

O God, our help in ages past
Isaac Watts (1674–1748)

O God, our help in ages past,
　　Our hope for years to come,
Our shelter from the stormy blast,
　　And our eternal home:

Under the shadow of thy throne
　　Thy saints have dwelt secure;
Sufficient is thine arm alone,
　　And our defence is sure.

Before the hills in order stood,
　　Or earth received her frame,
From everlasting thou art God,
　　To endless years the same.

A thousand ages in thy sight
　　Are like an evening gone,
Short as the watch that ends the night
　　Before the rising sun.

The busy tribes of flesh and blood,
　　With all their cares and fears,
Are carried downward by the flood,
　　And lost in following years.

Time, like an ever-rolling stream,
　　Bears all its sons away;
They fly forgotten, as a dream
　　Dies at the opening day.

O God, our help in ages past,
　　Our hope for years to come,
Be thou our guard while troubles last,
　　And our eternal home.

Isaac Watts was a great poet. He was passionate about his art, as one can see by reading some of his writings on the subject, such as his poem 'The Adventurous Muse', which condemns poetic timidity and celebrates poetic inspiration. When he wrote hymns he was more careful, but just as skilful. We can see this in the way in which a hymn like this is made: like a piece of furniture made by a master, the lines are perfectly shaped and jointed. Each verse is an exact and precise unit, sliding into its place like a well-made drawer in a cabinet; and all the drawers fit together into the whole unit, so that while every part is exactly and beautifully made, the whole is a joy to behold.

Take the words 'help' and 'hope' in the first verse. They are close together in sound, yet far apart in meaning, so that the mind takes them in as similar yet different. 'Help' belongs to the past; 'hope' to the future. The hymn looks back and looks forward, from 'in ages past' to 'in years to come'; and then back again, recalling past troubles, 'the stormy blast', and forward again, looking to the future life, 'our eternal home'.

The perspective of this hymn is vast. It moves from all that we can remember of the past to all that we can hope for in the future. And because of this it is about time. Time is how we measure our lives, in hours, days, months, years, so that the hymn is a perpetual reminder of the human condition. Indeed, its first title was 'Man frail, and God eternal', and it is based on Psalm 90, the magnificent statement of the greatness of God and the littleness of human beings. In the psalm, and in this metrical version of it, the greatness of God is described in terms of time: God was there before the hills, and before the earth was shaped, and a thousand years in his sight are like an evening, or like the short watch before the dawn breaks.

In its description of God's grandeur, the hymn makes us think of the sublime features of nature. In our mind's eye we see a range of hills, standing 'in order', in their place where they have been for millions of years. Any geologist will tell you that our recent history, over the last ten thousand years, is but a tiny fragment of the huge span of geological ages; and the hymn tells us that God existed before that. It challenges our powers of thinking: it is hard even to imagine – as it should be. Which of us has any right to think that they can know God? Or as God himself said to Job,

Where wast thou when I laid the foundations of the earth?
Whereupon are the foundations thereof fastened? Or who laid the
  corner stone thereof;
When the morning stars sang together, and all the sons of God
  shouted for joy?

(Job 38.4, 6–7)

This is a stern reminder of the limits of human understanding
and of the greatness of God, of the huge distance between Job and
the Creator of the universe.

As a contrast to the almost unimaginable timelessness of God,
this hymn invites us to consider the shortness of human life. The
Venerable Bede gave an example in his *History of the English Church
and People*: think of a sparrow, he said to the king, that flies into
your hall through one door and then out through another. This is
like the life of men and women, a brief passage from the winter
outside into the warmth and light of the hall, and then out into
the winter again. We see the sparrow for a moment, 'but of what
follows or what went before, we are utterly ignorant'. Like many
of the stories from that early period of Christianity, this one has a
profound meaning. It finds an echo in this hymn, which follows
the psalm as it turns from the greatness of God to the shortness
of human life. 'The busy tribes of flesh and blood' are carried
downstream, generation after generation, like so many pieces of
flotsam. They disappear into the distance, carried away by the
never-ceasing processes of time. Time is inexorable and undeviating
in its onward course: people live, and then die, and are remembered for a time, and then (unless they are famous) gradually
forgotten. They become faces in a photograph album, when no
one can remember their names any more. One day, of course, it
will all vanish, as Shakespeare saw:

The cloud capp'd towers, the gorgeous palaces,
The solemn temples, the great globe itself,
Yea, all which it inherit, shall dissolve,
And, like this insubstantial pageant faded,
Leave not a rack behind. We are such stuff
As dreams are made on; and our little life
Is rounded with a sleep.

(*The Tempest*)

I have sometimes wondered if this image was in Watts's mind, when he wrote

> Time, like an ever-rolling stream,
>   Bears all its sons away;
> They fly forgotten, as a dream
>   Dies at the opening day.

The word 'time' here is like a bell, or a sudden strong chord in music. This is what Watts has been talking about since the beginning, but only now does he bring it out into the open. It is time, the old enemy, that steals away our early years, 'that subtle thief of youth', as Milton called it; then our middle age; and then life itself. As the old cricketer's poem has it, 'Time takes the wicket, death begins to bowl.' The weathercock at Lord's Cricket Ground, with Father Time taking off the bails, is an apt symbol: like the umpire, drawing stumps at the end of the day, time declares that the match is over. You have had your innings.

Faced with this prospect, what should our response be? Watts is in no doubt: it is prayer. In the last verse he returns to the opening, with its help in the past and its hope for the future, but then he alters the last two lines, so that they become a prayer to God. His response to the human situation that he has delineated so powerfully – a little life, a fading dream, humanity frail and God eternal – is:

> Be thou our guard while troubles last,
>   And our eternal home.

The prayer is for this world and the next, 'While troubles last' (earth) and 'our eternal home' (heaven). It is a prayer that we may live protected by God on earth, and that we may come at last to his eternal joy in heaven.

This hymn is as powerful as any tragedy in its depiction of the realities of human existence. As one of the characters in Samuel Beckett's *Waiting for Godot* says, 'They give birth astride of a grave, the light gleams an instant, then it's night once more.' The Christian response to this is not to despair, or to try to avoid this human condition; but to pray for help in this life, and to hope for heaven in the next. Help and hope are the twin responses that help us to make sense of the frailty and shortness of our little lives.

God moves in a mysterious way
William Cowper (1731–1800)

God moves in a mysterious way
   His wonders to perform;
He plants his footsteps in the sea,
   And rides upon the storm.

Deep in unfathomable mines
   Of never-failing skill,
He treasures up his bright designs,
   And works his sovereign will.

Ye fearful saints, fresh courage take;
   The clouds ye so much dread
Are big with mercy, and shall break
   In blessings on your head.

Judge not the Lord by feeble sense,
   But trust him for his grace;
Behind a frowning providence
   He hides a smiling face.

His purposes will ripen fast,
   Unfolding every hour;
The bud may have a bitter taste,
   But sweet will be the flower.

Blind unbelief is sure to err,
   And scan his work in vain;
God is his own interpreter,
   And he will make it plain.

William Cowper was a distinguished eighteenth-century poet, whose hymns reflect much of his sensitivity and tender feeling. They were written for the most part at Olney in Buckinghamshire during a brief period of collaboration with his friend John

Newton. The little summer house where they worked in the garden can be seen to this day. In his later years Cowper suffered much from depression, but for a short time between 1767 and 1773 he enjoyed a peace of mind that enabled him to turn his considerable poetic skill to the writing of hymns. They were published, together with those of Newton, in *Olney Hymns* (1779), a book which became a classic of evangelical spirituality.

This hymn was written shortly before Cowper had a serious depressive illness in 1773, but it shows no sign of the unhappiness which was to come. It breathes a calm assurance and serenity, while at the same time acknowledging that God's purposes are difficult for us to comprehend. What is interesting about it is that it is not just a hymn of praise to the Creator: it is not like, for example, 'O worship the King'. It is about the problems that we face when we contemplate the purposes of God in the world. Sometimes they seem incomprehensible. But the whole movement of the hymn is from the word 'mysterious' in the first line to the word 'plain' in the last one.

The word 'plain' does not mean that everything becomes easier. We never come any closer to an understanding of God's ways. It is he who will make it plain, because he alone is the interpreter (this comes from Genesis 40.8, when Joseph says, 'Do not interpretations belong to God?'). What we can do is hold fast to belief; we have to understand that God may have a purpose which is often not understood. This was a popular theory in Cowper's day: that, however incomprehensible God's ways were, they must be right. In *An Essay on Man* (1730–2) Alexander Pope stated it clearly:

All Nature is but Art, unknown to thee;
All Chance, Direction, which thou canst not see;
All Discord, Harmony not understood;
All partial Evil, universal Good:
And, spite of Pride, in erring Reason's spite,
One truth is clear, 'Whatever IS, is RIGHT.'

Pope was attacking human pride, and the idea that the possession of reason gave human beings the right to think that they knew about God. Whatever happened must be part of God's plan, even though we cannot see it. This idea has many drawbacks: it was put under great pressure in 1755 when an earthquake in Lisbon destroyed much of the city and killed many thousands of people; and again in 2004 when a tidal wave struck the sea-coasts of South-East Asia. Its one great merit is that it puts human beings in their place. In the light of such horrendous natural disasters, it is natural to question the loving purposes of God, but when we do so we are assuming that he is somehow like us. Against this we must set the words of the psalmist:

> He bowed the heavens also, and came down: and darkness was under his feet. And he rode upon a cherub, and did fly: yea, he did fly upon the wings of the wind. He made darkness his secret place; his pavilion round about him were dark waters and thick clouds of the skies. (Psalm 18.9–11)

The awe and majesty of God is celebrated everywhere in the psalms. 'The heavens declare the glory of God; and the firmament sheweth his handywork' (Psalm 19.1). The proper response to this is humility: 'When I consider thy heavens, the work of thy fingers, the moon and the stars, which thou hast ordained; What is man, that thou art mindful of him?' (Psalm 8).

In our modern times, we do not like to think of God in this way. We call God 'you', as if this will somehow make him more accessible and friendly (so that when something like the Asian tsunami comes, we feel bewildered). Cowper's hymn is a valuable corrective. It echoes the psalms in its poetic imagery of splendour, with God as some giant figure striding the waves:

> He plants his footsteps in the sea,
> And rides upon the storm.

Storms are dangerous, but God may be in them. Equally difficult to comprehend is that sometimes God's beautiful creativity seems wasted, because no one will see it. If he is a giant in verse 1, he is a craftsman in verse 2, but in both cases we should not try to rationalize what he is doing, 'deep in unfathomable mines'.

But wait, says Cowper; what seem to be incomprehensible circumstances may turn out better than we think. Being a man who loved walking in the fields and paths near Olney, he uses the image of the rain cloud:

> The clouds ye so much dread
> Are big with mercy, and shall break
> In blessings on your head.

He must have been thinking of the English weather, the change-able mixture of clouds and sunshine that makes walkers carry umbrellas; although the imagery itself is from Portia's eloquent courtroom speech in *The Merchant of Venice*:

> The quality of mercy is not strained;
> It droppeth as the gentle rain from heaven . . .

The crucial word in both texts is 'mercy'. God's ways, we know, are unfathomable, and he is an awe-inspiring figure, but just when we are fearful, suddenly, the cloud bursts and the rain falls. Ezekiel wrote of it (34.26): 'there shall be showers of blessing'. It was the source of the old gospel hymn:

> Showers of blessing,
> Showers of blessing we need;
> Mercy-drops round us are falling,
> But for the showers we plead.

We now see how effective Cowper's technique has been. After two verses that build up the idea of God as terrible, the relief of his mercy is wonderful. It falls in rain, not in a few raindrops. And from this point on the hymn goes on to assert the goodness of God: 'Behind a frowning providence / He hides a smiling face.' The frown is like a mask here, which is snatched off, as in a child's game, to reveal a smile. Similarly, the bud, which tastes bitter, gives way to the flower; and God's purposes unfold and ripen, like a plant in the sunshine.

So Cowper asserts that there is a hidden purpose in God's ways, or a purpose that will ultimately be revealed. We cannot under-stand it, sometimes, but it is there. This is no comfort to those who have suffered from natural disasters, or undeserved illness and sorrow, but it is an important reminder that human beings have limits to their understanding: 'What is man, that thou art mindful of him?' We should obviously use our minds, for the intellect is God-given, one of the glories of our human life. But there is a danger, as Pope saw, that 'erring Reason' would main-tain that God does not exist. To this the psalmist also had an answer: 'The fool hath said in his heart, There is no God' (Psalm 53.1). Cowper calls this 'blind unbelief', which is 'sure to err'. His hymn, more gently and compassionately, says the same thing.

Rock of Ages, cleft for me
Augustus Montague Toplady
(1740–78)

Rock of Ages, cleft for me,
Let me hide myself in thee;
Let the Water and the Blood,
From the riven side which flowed,
Be of sin the double cure,
Cleanse me from its guilt and power.

Not the labours of my hands
Can fulfil thy law's demands;
Could my zeal no respite know,
Could my tears for ever flow,
All for sin could not atone;
Thou must save, and thou alone.

Nothing in my hand I bring,
Simply to the cross I cling;
Naked, come to thee for dress;
Helpless, look to thee for grace;
Foul, I to the fountain fly;
Wash me, Saviour, or I die.

Whilst I draw this fleeting breath,
When mine eyes are closed in death,
When I soar through tracts unknown,
See thee on thy judgment throne;
Rock of ages, cleft for me,
Let me hide myself in thee.

How does one explain the effect of a hymn such as this? It is not just the words, or the tunes, fine though they are, both the English and the American tunes; it is something to do with an almost magical combination of sound, rhythm and imagery, all of which come together to answer to a kind of yearning in the soul. The singing of this hymn is an expression of a very human need for reassurance, for safety and security; and in spiritual terms, it acknowledges sin and preaches salvation.

Augustus Montague Toplady, who wrote the hymn in 1775, held to the beliefs of a Calvinist: that human beings were imperfect and prone to sin, and that they could be saved from sin and hell only by the grace of God in Jesus Christ. In this view, all are sinners, and there is no hope for us in attempting to win God's favour by good works. Our hope has to be in the saving action of Christ on the cross, rather than in any actions of our own. We are justified by faith and not by works. This doctrine of 'justification by faith' is based on the discussion of the relative merits of faith and works in St Paul's Epistle to the Romans. From Luther and Calvin onwards, it has been a fundamental element of Protestant belief, though modified by some important figures such as John Wesley, who insisted that faith should lead to good works (and who quarrelled with Toplady on this matter).

This hymn presents the Calvinist doctrine of faith rather than works in its clearest form: 'Not the labours of my hands / Can fulfil thy law's demands.' The only solution is 'Thou must save, and thou alone.' It is a very bold statement, but one which is echoed by many hymns which emphasize the importance of faith: 'The vilest offender that truly believes / That moment from Jesus a pardon receives.'

The jogtrot of that jingle, by Fanny Crosby, serves as a contrast to Toplady's majestic sound: 'Rock of Ages, cleft for me'. Toplady's line sounds huge and powerful. The image of the rock goes back to the Old Testament, when Moses was told, 'I will put thee in a clift of the rock, and will cover thee with my hand' (Exodus 33.22). But this is not just a rock, but the 'Rock of Ages', ancient rock, prehuman rock, the rock that is a symbol of God himself: the phrase takes us back to the Ancient of Days, the God who is as hard as rock, the God who in the last verse appears on his 'judgment throne'.

But now that rock is 'cleft for me'. Something has happened to the rock, so that it becomes no longer a hard presence, granite-like in its solidity, but a protection. The rock is cleft by the sacrifice of Christ: God himself, the righteous judge, is also the merciful one, the Christ who has provided the shelter from the wrath of God. The idea of hiding in the cleft of a rock is very powerful. It takes us back to something primitive within us. In his book, *The Experience of Landscape*, Jay Appleton analyses the response to landscape in terms of what he calls the 'prospect-refuge' theory. In earliest times, our ancestors needed landscapes which either allowed them to see a long way, to see animals or the approach of enemies (prospect), or landscape that permitted them to hide from danger (refuge). The landscape of this hymn is a refuge landscape. It has given rise to the story (thought not to be true) that Toplady wrote the hymn in a cave in the Cheddar Gorge in Somerset while sheltering from a thunderstorm.

It is easy to see how such a story might have come about. For the last lines of the hymn repeat the first lines, and emphasize the wish to hide from the wrath of God's judgement in the cleft of the rock. It is what happens in between that transforms the mystery of the first two lines into meaningful metaphor. We begin the hymn, not quite knowing what these marvellous lines might mean; we end it with some understanding of what the cleft in the rock, and the rock itself, are about. Suddenly, in the third line of verse 1, we have not hardness, but fluidity, the water and blood that flowed from the side of the crucified Jesus. They are two elements, and thus a 'double cure'. They cleanse us from two things: the guilt that we feel about sin, and its power over us.

Verse 2 is a dramatic statement of the doctrine of justification by faith. All the zeal, all the tears, all the works ('the labours of my hands') are of no avail: 'Thou must save, and thou alone.' The force comes into the poetry because Toplady feels it applied to himself: 'Rock of Ages, cleft for *me*'. So in verse 3 he comes to the cross as he is, naked, helpless and dirty: he prays to be dressed, to be helped by grace, and to be made clean, washed in the fountain of living water. The last line sums up his own need of cleansing: 'Wash me, Saviour, or I die.' Everything is dependent on Christ.

The last verse speaks of life and of death. It puts everything that has gone before into the context of our short life and of what will happen to us after death. In that context the fate of the individual soul becomes a matter of vital importance. Life is a short time in which to draw breath – 'this fleeting breath' – and then comes death, the closing of our eyes in the last sleep (Toplady actually wrote 'when my eye-strings break in death', because the tendons behind the eyes were thought to break at the moment of death). Then, says Toplady, the soul soars through tracts unknown, finding its way to the throne of judgement. Then it pleads for mercy through the blood of Christ, the sacrificial Lamb who has cleft the rock for us and given us the water of life.

Because of its dramatic landscapes and its concentration on the individual 'me', this hymn has a tremendous force. It places the human being in the centre of a cosmic spiritual geology: before him is the rock, and in it is the cleft of the rock. He prays to be allowed to hide in the cleft because he knows that he is at the centre of a world in which judgement is certain and the cross his only hope. He moves through the landscape, conscious of his own unworthiness, clinging to the cross as to a lifebelt in the sea, naked, dirty and helpless. It is a picture which goes to the heart of the human condition. It asks, as Dietrich Bonhoeffer was later to ask, 'Who am I?' And it answers: 'Nothing, without the mercy of God in Jesus Christ.' Bonhoeffer's heroism, his imprisonment and martyrdom at the hands of the Nazis has inspired generations since his death in 1945; his poem contrasts his calm outward appearance, the way he is seen by others, with the inner self that he alone knows, 'restless and longing and sick, like a bird in a cage'. In it, he never finds an answer to his question 'Who am I? This or the other?' – the confident man his fellow-prisoners see, or the weary and restless self that he alone knows. His conclusion is:

> Who am I? They mock me, these lonely questions of mine.
> Whoever I am, Thou knowest, O God, I am thine!

Toplady's answer to the question 'Who am I?' would be that he is the sinner who is saved by the blood of Jesus Christ. He prays to the Christ, as God Incarnate, to be allowed to hide in the cleft of the rock that is his salvation. This is his answer: he is nothing without that redemption, just as Bonhoeffer's questions about his own selfhood end in the one answer that he *can* be sure about: 'I am thine.'

Dear Lord and Father of mankind
John Greenleaf Whittier (1807–92)

Dear Lord and Father of mankind,
  Forgive our foolish ways;
Reclothe us in our rightful mind;
In purer lives thy service find,
  In deeper reverence, praise.

In simple trust like theirs who heard
  Beside the Syrian sea
The gracious calling of the Lord,
Let us, like them, without a word
  Rise up and follow thee.

O Sabbath rest by Galilee!
  O calm of hills above,
Where Jesus knelt to share with thee
The silence of eternity,
  Interpreted by love!

With that deep hush subduing all
  Our words and works that drown
The tender whisper of thy call,
As noiseless let thy blessing fall
  As fell thy manna down.

Drop thy still dews of quietness,
  Till all our strivings cease;
Take from our souls the strain and stress,
And let our ordered lives confess
  The beauty of thy peace.

Breathe through the heats of our desire
  Thy coolness and thy balm;
Let sense be dumb, let flesh retire,

Speak through the earthquake, wind, and fire,
  O still small voice of calm!

This is a hymn for all occasions. It is very popular for weddings, just as 'The day thou gavest, Lord, is ended' is popular for funerals. The two hymns have this in common: neither was intended for the occasions for which they are now used. Of course, there is no reason why a hymn such as this should not be 'taken over' and used for a wedding; if it pleases those who are taking part, then that must be a good thing. And this hymn is certainly very beautiful, especially when it is sung to the tune Repton by Sir Hubert Parry. Its mood of quiet devotion can be very well suited to the solemnity of a marriage service, before the celebrations afterwards.

It had a very unusual beginning. It was written by a distinguished American poet and man of letters, the New England Quaker John Greenleaf Whittier. He was a man of strong views and high principles, who was a passionate opponent of slavery. Whittier was somewhat sceptical of religion without moral action: in one of his poems, 'The Sabbath Scene', a runaway slave takes refuge in a church, only to be handed back by the minister and congregation to his owner. Whittier's fury is clear:

'Is this', I cried,
  'The end of prayer and preaching?
Then down with pulpit, down with priest,
  And give us nature's teaching!'

In 'Dear Lord and Father of mankind' he was writing about something different: church services. He liked worship to be devout, simple, serious, quiet, and reflective, and he preferred the Quaker silence to all other forms. When he did write about worship, it was to question the way in which it could be ritual or formal without impinging upon everyday life:

Our Friend, our Brother, and our Lord,
  What may thy service be?
Nor name, nor form, nor ritual word,
  But simply following thee.

The poem from which this comes, 'Our Master', contains verses from which we have the hymn 'Immortal Love, for ever full', and this is typical of Whittier's hymns: they are almost always made up of selected verses from longer poems. 'Dear Lord and Father of mankind' is a good example. These six verses are from a very peculiar poem called 'The Brewing of Soma'. Soma is an Indian plant that was used as a drug in some religious services, where it induced a state of intoxication and frenzy in those who took it to excess. Whittier read about this plant and its uses, and saw a parallel with what he thought was a growing tendency for church services in his own day to become noisy and excitable. So he used the idea of the brewing of soma to identify what he saw as worship that distracted from the contemplation of the truly serious things of life. He described what he called 'some fever of the blood and brain', which he associated with all kinds of ritual, including 'music, incense, vigils drear' which, as a Quaker, he distrusted:

> In sensual transports wild as vain
> We brew in many a Christian fane
>   The heathen Soma still!

It is at this point that, after several verses of angry condemnation, the reader suddenly comes across the tranquil beauty of:

> Dear Lord and Father of mankind
>   Forgive our foolish ways . . .

Now that it has been detached from its strange origins, this hymn – the last six verses of the poem – becomes a general plea for forgiveness and for a better future. The prayer 'Reclothe us in our rightful mind' leads towards purer and better lives, and to a deeper reverence before God. The pattern for this change is the calling of the apostles from their work beside the sea of Galilee. They followed Jesus 'without a word'. It is true that they said nothing, or nothing that is recorded in the Bible; but here it also suggests that they quietly left what they were doing and followed him without making a fuss about it – 'simply following thee'.

What followed for the apostles was a time of difficulty, self-surrender, privation and even suffering; but the third verse chooses to describe something else in their lives: a moment of supreme beauty and calm, one of those moments which must have cheered them and made them realize that they were in the presence of someone whose life was hidden with God. That verse describes a moment of great natural beauty: there is the sea of Galilee, with the hills beyond, in the quietness of the Sabbath, and Jesus kneeling with them in prayer. It must have been a time of memorable inspiration, one of those moments in which it all seemed worthwhile, and one of those times which gave the apostles strength to carry on. So it is for us, says Whittier; we too could find strength in such moments, but too often they are drowned, or crowded out, by 'our words and works', that everyday busy-ness of our normal existence.

The fourth verse is a plea for quietness, and for the attentive ear; and the image of the dew and manna falling on the children of Israel is a powerful reminder of the gentle providence of God, which provided for the Israelites silently while they were asleep (Exodus 16). This is applied to ourselves at the beginning of the next verse, with 'Drop thy still dews of quietness'; like spiritual manna, God will quietly deliver peace to us if we pray for it. Our souls will lose their strain and stress; our lives, no longer confused and aimless, will become ordered.

The beauty of God's peace leads into the final verse, with its reference to the still small voice which spoke to Elijah (from 1 Kings 19.12). God's voice was not in the earthquake, the wind, or the fire, but in the quietness, the still small voice of calm. It is important that the last word of the hymn should be 'calm', for the whole hymn has been leading up to it. It is one of the ideas that has run through the hymn and created its atmosphere – 'simple trust', 'Sabbath rest', 'calm of hills above', 'deep hush', 'tender whisper', 'still dews of quietness', 'thy coolness and thy balm'. The cumulative effect of these words is to create an effect that is soothing, calming, cooling (as opposed to 'the heats of our desire'), bringing before us the idea of 'the beauty of thy peace'.

It is this which accounts for the appeal of this hymn. It does not just *tell* us to look for beauty and peace, or to be quiet and listen for the quiet voice of God. Its words, its evenly paced lines, its verses set to Parry's lovely tune, all these make us *feel* the beauty as we sing. There is nothing discordant or even exciting in these lines; they make us feel restful and peaceful as we sing them. And because the tune requires the last line of each verse to be sung twice, the mind can take that line and dwell upon it, sink into it, before the next verse picks up the idea again.

It is easy to underestimate the enchantment of sound in worship, and the place of the imagination in it. The line 'O Sabbath rest by Galilee' is an example: it gives us a momentary picture of something that can exist in our minds as wonderful, whether it is true or not. The novelist D. H. Lawrence wrote about the same thing. Quoting 'O Galilee, sweet Galilee, / Come sing thy songs again to me', he went on:

> To me the word Galilee has a wonderful sound. The Lake of Galilee! I don't want to know where it is. I never want to go to Palestine. Galilee is one of those lovely, glamorous worlds, not places, that exist in the golden haze of a child's half-formed imagination. And in my man's imagination it is just the same.

He saw that the words themselves have their own mystery and magic; and we should never forget that what the hymn *says* is only part of the story. As with any poem, a hymn has an effect that goes far beyond its 'message'. By its beauty it leads us on to worlds that we can only dimly see. So it is no wonder that this hymn is often chosen for weddings: it opens the door to another world, a world of beauty and peace that is 'interpreted by love'. It takes us deeper and deeper into a state of mind in which we can be nobler as men and women, kinder to our fellow human beings, and in a closer relationship with God: in deeper reverence, we pray and praise.

Love divine, all loves excelling
Charles Wesley (1707–88)

Love Divine, all loves excelling,
   Joy of heaven, to earth come down,
Fix in us thy humble dwelling,
   All thy faithful mercies crown.
Jesu, thou art all compassion,
   Pure unbounded love thou art;
Visit us with thy salvation,
   Enter every trembling heart.

Come, almighty to deliver,
   Let us all thy life receive;
Suddenly return, and never,
   Never more thy temples leave.
Thee we would be always blessing,
   Serve thee as thy hosts above,
Pray, and praise thee, without ceasing,
   Glory in thy perfect love.

Finish then thy new creation,
   Pure and spotless let us be;
Let us see thy great salvation,
   Perfectly restored in thee:
Changed from glory into glory,
   Till in heaven we take our place,
Till we cast our crowns before thee,
   Lost in wonder, love, and praise!

Charles Wesley delighted in taking passages from the poetry of others and adapting them for his own purposes. Often a line from another poem gave him an idea for a hymn, even if the original poem was not Christian or religious at all. Indeed, it seems that he often preferred it that way: an idea or a phrase, on an entirely secular topic, could be taken and given a new (and Christian) life. It was as if the words themselves, hitherto part of a worldly sphere, could be themselves 'converted', taken and offered up as a gift to Christ.

This hymn is a good example. It begins by adapting words from an opera by Henry Purcell with a libretto by John Dryden, *King Arthur*, first performed in 1691. In Act II there is a 'Song sung by Venus in honour of Britannia', beginning

> Fairest Isle, all isles excelling,
> Seat of pleasures and of loves,
> Venus here will make her dwelling,
> And forsake her Cyprian groves.

The idea is that Venus, who was traditionally born in Cyprus and always associated with that island, will leave it and come to take up her home in Britain. This is because Britain is, in the song, the most beautiful of all islands and the 'seat of pleasures and of loves'. The two words, 'pleasures' and 'loves', suggest amorous delights, and of course Venus was the goddess of sexual love. Her Greek name, Aphrodite, gives us our own word 'aphrodisiac'. In some legends her son was the powerful god Eros, from which comes the word 'erotic'.

Charles Wesley was writing of another love. This is 'Love *divine*', and the word 'divine', which we often take for granted in this first line, is an important signal. It tells the reader that this is about an entirely different experience. I am writing, says Charles Wesley, about the love of God in Christ Jesus and not about profane or sexual love. Dryden and Purcell celebrated Britain as the seat of pleasure: I shall explore something finer, a love that excels all other loves.

So the important word in line 1 is 'divine'. The hymn then goes on to describe what that divine love might be. It is love itself which is 'the joy of heaven', the love that makes the angels rejoice and is the nearest that we mortals can get to an idea of what God is, for God is love. It is hard for mortals to think about heaven, but in any idea that we may have of it, love must be at the centre of it. As the poet W. H. Auden once wrote, love is 'the interest itself in thoughtless Heaven', in that glorious place where there are no 'thoughts' in the normal human sense. But if love is the joy and centre of heaven, Christians believe that love came to earth in the person of Jesus Christ. This is why Charles Wesley goes on with the phrase 'to earth come down'. It could be that he is saying 'Joy of heaven [which has] come down' (at the incarnation) or 'Joy of heaven [we pray] come down'. Either way it suggests that heavenly or divine love can come to earth, fixing its dwelling in the human heart, however humble and unworthy that may be. This is a tremendous and awe-inspiring possibility, and it is not surprising that the verse should end with 'trembling heart': this is the heart trembling to receive the salvation from above, the 'pure unbounded love'. If this love really did fix itself in the human heart, then that would indeed be the crowning mercy ('All thy faithful mercies crown').

There is a beautiful story told by the Latin poet Ovid in his *Metamorphoses* Book VIII, in which Jupiter and Mercury come to earth disguised as mortals. They look for rest and food, but are turned away from a thousand homes. Eventually they come to a poor cottage, where they are kindly received by an old couple, Baucis and Philemon, who stir up the cooking fire, set out somewhere for the visitors to sit, and get out some cabbage and bacon. They clean and lay the table: because one leg is too short it has to be propped up with a tile. They lay out the food, and try to catch their one goose to feed the guests. Then they notice that the wine bowl keeps filling up of its own accord; the goose flees for refuge to the visitors; and then Jupiter and Mercury reveal themselves as two of the gods. The inhospitable people of the neighbourhood are drowned by a flood, while Baucis and Philemon's house is turned into a beautiful temple. The gods offer the old couple any boon they care to choose: they decide that when their time comes they would like to die in the same hour. This prayer is granted, and they just have time to say, 'Farewell, dear loved one' before they are turned into graceful trees, standing in front of the temple.

Charles Wesley would have known this story from his school-days, and I think he used it in this hymn. The love of God in the world is its theme, the hope that all mankind may be delivered from sin and given life, and that God will 'Suddenly return, and never, / Never more thy temples leave.' Like Baucis and Philemon in Ovid's story, the hymn asks for a boon. Like them, we 'would [wish to] be' always serving God:

> Thee we would be always blessing,
>> Serve thee as thy hosts above,
> Pray, and praise thee, without ceasing,
>> Glory in thy perfect love.

But this is not the end of the story. The third verse begins on earth, with the 'great salvation' of humankind, but ends in heaven. It begins with St Paul telling the Corinthians that 'if any man be in Christ, he is a new creature' (2 Corinthians 5.17). Possessed of the divine love, we shall be like him, which is what Wesley is aiming for. He began the hymn by telling us about divine love. Now he raises the possibility that we can be transformed by it, just as Baucis and Philemon were transformed by the gods. If we take that divine love into ourselves, we can be 'thy new creation'; just as God finished the first creation in six days, so now we pray that we may be 'finished', that any longings and stumbling after goodness (starting the process, we might say) may be taken by Christ and finished. It is a tremendous prospect, that we might be like him, but others have thought it before: Ireneaus, who lived in the second century, wrote of the Incarnate God 'who for his immense love's sake was made that which we are, in order that he might perfect us to be what he is'. If this 'immense love', Wesley's 'love divine', is within us, then we can truly be changed, and heaven awaits, glory upon glory:

> Changed from glory into glory,
>   Till in heaven we take our place,
> Till we cast our crowns before thee,
>   Lost in wonder, love, and praise!

We are lost in this vision: it is so magnificent that we find ourselves totally unlike our normal selves. We have a sudden vision of ourselves, yet not ourselves, casting down our crowns before the throne of God like the four and twenty elders in Revelation 4.10. If we are supremely fortunate, if we lose ourselves and empty ourselves of all but divine love, we can find ourselves before the throne of God himself, filled with wonder, love and praise. And if this is normally not possible, if the daily cares of human life press too closely upon us, then the possibility and the hope can still be there. Most of us can feel that there is a possibility, just a possibility, that we might be transformed by the mysteries and mercies of divine love into someone worthy to stand before the throne of God. And certainly, we can experience that feeling, however briefly, when singing this hymn.

How sweet the name of Jesus sounds
John Newton (1725–1807)

How sweet the name of Jesus sounds
  In a believer's ear!
It soothes his sorrows, heals his wounds,
  And drives away his fear.

It makes the wounded spirit whole,
  And calms the troubled breast;
'Tis manna to the hungry soul,
  And to the weary rest.

Dear name! the rock on which I build,
  My shield and hiding place,
My never-failing treasury, filled
  With boundless stores of grace!

Jesus! my Shepherd, Brother, Friend,
  My Prophet, Priest, and King.
My Lord, my Life, my Way, my End,
  Accept the praise I bring.

Weak is the effort of my heart,
  And cold my warmest thought;
But when I see thee as thou art,
  I'll praise thee as I ought.

Till then I would thy love proclaim
  With every fleeting breath;
And may the music of thy name
  Refresh my soul in death.

The author of this hymn had a most extraordinary life. He went
to sea as a young man, wild and godless, and lived the hard life of

a seaman, rising to become a captain and working among the terrible cruelties of the slave trade. He was close to death in a great storm with a leaky ship on one occasion, and must have endured hardships at sea that would make most normal people quail. On leaving the slave trade, Newton settled in Liverpool, where he came under the influence of the evangelist George White-field and of John Wesley. He became a clergyman, first at Olney in Buckinghamshire, and then at St Mary Woolnoth in the City of London, where there is a touching memorial tablet to him. Even after death, his unusual life continued: to make Bank Underground Station, the bodies in the graveyard of St Mary Woolnoth had to be dug up and reinterred, so that Newton's remains now rest in the churchyard at Olney.

At Olney, Newton had the poet William Cowper in his congregation, and the two collaborated to produce *Olney Hymns* in 1779. Newton was clearly the stronger personality of the two, and his hymns are more numerous, and generally more vigorous, than Cowper's. Sometimes they reflect his old seafaring life, as in 'Begone unbelief, / My Saviour is near', in which he boldly says 'With Christ in the vessel / I smile at the storm'. The present hymn is one of his gentler ones: the word 'sweet' in the first line is carefully chosen. It introduces a hymn that has been a source of comfort for many, and quite rightly. It speaks from the outset of 'the name of Jesus' as a talisman that (1) soothes sorrows, (2) heals wounds, and (3) drives away fear. One, two, three: the troubles of this world are banished, one by one. The hymn sweeps us off our feet with its splendid opening confidence.

The second verse carefully and majestically expands on this. The name of Jesus heals the wounded spirit, calms the troubled breast, feeds the hungry soul and gives rest to the weary. One, two, three, four: the assurance of the first verse is continued and even expanded. The sorrows / wounds / fear of the first verse had external causes. Now the problems turn inwards, to the inner-most parts of the soul: they are the wounded spirit, the troubled breast, the hungry soul, and the weariness of life. Each of these, except perhaps the last, is a condition which owes little to the out-side world, but which is the result of inner conflicts. It is the spirit which is wounded, the breast which is troubled, and the soul which is hungry. It is a comprehensive picture of a soul which is in despair, confused, and desperate for spiritual food. Without spiritual manna, the soul will perish, as the children of Israel would have done in the wilderness without real manna.

What Newton is doing here is summing up the human condition. We live in a fallen world, and we are conscious that we have to endure its imperfections: the loss of loved ones, tragic accidents, terrible natural disasters, ill-health and disease; and other things too – disappointment, unfairness, failure, anger, fear. Things cannot always be as we would like them to be; and we have to endure them with whatever fortitude we can summon up. To all of these troubles, Newton opposes the consolations of religion. Whatever happens, there are the words of Jesus: 'In the world ye shall have tribulation: but be of good cheer; I have overcome the world' (John 16.33). Newton had experienced this in his own life, and now he passes it on to others.

Similarly the second verse ends with the beautiful line, 'And to the weary rest', which is a reminder of 'Come unto me, all ye that labour and are heavy laden, and I will give you rest' (Matthew 11.28). This could be addressed to anyone who has enduring problems: long-term illness, the daily duty of care, the loneliness of those who find themselves unloved. Newton's hymn is acutely aware of the troubles of this world, but his first two verses end on that consoling word 'rest'. It is like the vision of Christina Rossetti that the road winds 'up-hill all the way', which ends with the welcome at the inn:

> Will there be beds for me and all who seek?
> Yea, beds for all who come.

From the promise of rest, Newton turns to the joys of religion: the name of Jesus is a rock on which to build his defence against the world, and a treasure-house of grace. To him, as a sinner, is vouchsafed the grace of forgiveness: that grace is stored in a treasury that never fails. And so now he celebrates: shepherd, brother, friend, prophet, priest, king. The nouns pile on top of one another in a joyful series of names, almost as if Newton were shouting them, one after another. The mind has no time to take in the full implications of each: it just registers each one as part of this many-sided nature, this Saviour who is all these things, and more. He is 'my Lord, my Life, my Way, my End', which is taken from

John 14.6: 'I am the way, the truth, and the life', and repeated by the poet, so that he answers and affirms, 'You *are* my way, my truth, my life'. It is an acknowledgement of the claim of Jesus himself, but also an appropriate completion of the *wholeness* of Jesus, which is what these two verses have been about. What they are saying, in image after image, is that Jesus Christ is all, and in all. He is 'my End', that is to say my goal, the truth towards which I journey, the end of all things. It is as if the verse is now complete, but that it has shown us many sides, as if holding up a many-sided piece of glass or crystal, and turning it to catch the light; yet being aware also that the glass is one very beautiful object.

That sense of an 'End' suggests also the end of life: when the hymn finishes, it does so on the word 'death'. Newton says in the last two verses that he will praise his Saviour for the rest of his life ('with every fleeting breath'), although his praise will be weak and cold on this earth. The praise will be given properly in heaven: 'when I see thee as thou art, / I'll praise thee as I ought.' So, suddenly, we realize that the word 'death' in the last line means 'life', because death is the gateway to life eternal. As the poet prays that the name of Jesus may refresh his soul on his deathbed, so he promises to praise him in the hereafter.

It is a hymn of trust, and belief, and comfort. In it John Newton, the old slave trader, accepts Christ as his Saviour and celebrates the joy that comes with it. He does not forget that in this world there are many troubles and tribulations, but these are overwhelmed by the great emotion that he is proclaiming here with such confidence. It expresses the course of his own life, from rough sailor to evangelical preacher. The hymn is a classic expression of the eighteenth-century religious revival, which brought Newton from a careless and godless youth to the feet of his Saviour.

Christ, whose glory fills the skies
Charles Wesley (1707–88)

Christ, whose glory fills the skies,
   Christ, the true, the only light,
Sun of Righteousness, arise,
   Triumph o'er the shades of night;
Day-spring from on high, be near;
Day-star, in my heart appear.

Dark and cheerless is the morn
   Unaccompanied by thee;
Joyless is the day's return,
   Till thy mercy's beams I see,
Till they inward light impart,
Glad my eyes, and warm my heart.

Visit then this soul of mine,
   Pierce the gloom of sin and grief;
Fill me, radiancy divine,
   Scatter all my unbelief;
More and more thyself display,
Shining to the perfect day.

One of the great religious pictures of the nineteenth century was William Holman Hunt's 'The Light of the World'. In it Christ, carrying a lantern, knocks at the door in what seems to be a dark wood. The door has not been opened for many years: thistles and ivy are growing up it. Nor can it be opened from the outside, for there is no door handle. It has to be opened from the inside. The moral is clear: Christ, who carries the light through the darkness, is appealing to the individual soul. It was inspired by Revelation 3.20: 'Behold, I stand at the door, and knock: if any man hear my voice, and open the door, I will come in to him, and will sup with him, and he with me.' Charles Wesley's hymn is also about Christ as the light of the world, and the darkness of sin and unbelief:

> Visit then this soul of mine.
>> Pierce the gloom of sin and grief;
> Fill me, radiancy divine,
>> Scatter all my unbelief.

The coming of Christ into the world was just such a light in the darkness, as we know from the opening chapter of St John's Gospel. The Word was with God, and the Word was God, and then the Word became flesh:

> In him was life; and the life was the light of men.
> And the light shineth in darkness; and the darkness
> comprehended it not.

The chapter goes on to describe John himself, 'a man sent from God':

> The same came for a witness, to bear witness of the Light, that all
>> men through him might believe.
> He was not that Light, but was sent to bear witness of that Light.
> That was the true Light, which lighteth every man that cometh
>> into the world.
> He was in the world, and the world was made by him, and the
>> world knew him not.
> He came unto his own, and his own received him not.
> But as many as received him, to them gave he power to become
>> the sons of God, even to them that believe on his name.

The familiar beauty of the words carries contrasts which are fundamental to our human existence: between light and darkness, between ingratitude and gratitude ('the world was made by him, and the world knew him not'), between receiving and rejecting ('his own received him not'), between believing and not believing.

This hymn also works through these basic oppositions. Not only is it a very beautiful hymn to sing (James Montgomery described it as 'one of Charles Wesley's loveliest progeny') but it has its roots in our most basic human needs: the preference for light over darkness, the longing for a better self, the need for a set of values by which to live. All these are part of the light which Wesley prays for: the beams of mercy, the scattering of unbelief, the company of Christ himself.

This is the light which Wesley calls the 'Sun of Righteousness'. It is the Sun who is the Son (of God): the Sun, and Son, that is the life and light of the world. The phrase 'Sun of Righteousness' comes from Malachi 4.2: 'But unto you that fear my name shall the Sun of righteousness arise with healing in his wings.' The promised Messiah will come, says this final chapter of the Old Testament, rising like the sun, but bringing a new day, the day of righteousness. It is in this spirit that Charles Wesley addresses Christ, the Saviour whose glory 'fills the skies' like a beautiful sunrise, chasing the darkness away. The same image of dawn is found in Zacharias's great hymn of praise which we call the Benedictus – 'Blessed be the Lord God of Israel' – used at Morning Prayer. In St Luke's Gospel, chapter 1, from which it comes, at verses 76 to 79 Zacharias says that John will 'go before the face of the Lord to prepare his ways' and 'give knowledge of salvation unto his people by the remission of their sins':

> Through the tender mercy of our God; whereby the dayspring from on high hath visited us.
> To give light to them that sit in darkness and in the shadow of death, and to guide our feet into the way of peace.

The dayspring is the dawn, the coming of light, the banishing of darkness:

> Day-spring from on high, be near;
> Day-star, in my heart appear.

The important phrase here is 'in my heart'. Charles Wesley prays for the glory of the brightness to become an inward quality, just as it would if the door in Holman Hunt's picture were opened, and the figure with the lantern could come in. He asks for 'inward light', because without it all is dark and dreary:

> Dark and cheerless is the morn
> Unaccompanied by thee.

The prayer for inward light echoes Milton, whose great epic *Paradise Lost* tells the whole story of the fall and the redemption, from the eating of the apple in the Garden of Eden to the promise of redemption, which the archangel Michael foretells in the final book. At the opening of Book III Milton, who is about to describe heaven, celebrates light itself – 'Hail, holy light'. As he does so, he remembers that he is blind, in lines of great beauty and pathos:

> Thus with the year
> Seasons return, but not to me returns
> Day, or the sweet approach of ev'n or morn,
> Or sight of vernal bloom, or summer's rose,
> Or flocks, or herds, or human face divine . . .

He is deprived of all the things that go with the gift of sight, but prays for a different light:

> So much the rather thou celestial light
> Shine inward, and the mind through all her powers
> Irradiate, there plant eyes, all mist from thence
> Purge and disperse, that I may see and tell
> Of things invisible to mortal sight.

The blindness to earthly things may allow him special insight into heavenly things. Charles Wesley, who was no doubt remembering Milton here, asks to be given the same inward light. As the morning breaks and the darkness flees away, he prays to be filled with that light: without it, the dawn is not a glorious one, with the Sun / Son filling the skies, but dark and cheerless, like some rainy winter morning.

The simple opposites of light and darkness, of fine weather and bad weather, are part of the structure of this hymn. It associates the darkness with unbelief, with sin and grief, with an absence of joy. It associates Christ with the triumph over darkness and with radiance divine. With Christ we can have the sunlight 'shining to the perfect day'; without Christ we are condemned to a life of gloom.

The hymn is a prayer for each individual Christian, asking for that inward light which is the presence of God. But it can also be a prayer for the world. The symbol of the glorious day reaches out to others. On a fine day we experience the joy of it ourselves, but we enjoy sharing it with others: 'lovely day', we say to people we meet. Charles Wesley wanted nothing more than that others should feel the same joy that he felt, should find their own personal darkness disappearing, to be replaced by a glorious light. He clearly believed that if we were all filled with light then Christ would be displayed to the world in us. At Evensong every day, Charles Wesley would have said or sung the 'Nunc dimittis', from Luke 2.29–32, in which the aged Simeon gives thanks that he has lived to see the Christ child:

> For mine eyes have seen thy salvation,
> Which thou hast prepared before the face of all people;
> A light to lighten the Gentiles, and the glory of thy people Israel.

Simeon was quoting 'a light to the Gentiles' from Isaiah 42.6. His vision of the child Jesus is like that of Charles Wesley and of Holman Hunt. All of them seek for a light that will be inward but which will, in the end, fill the whole world with light, shining to the perfect day.

In the world which we see around us, such a vision may seem unattainable. The idea that 'the earth shall be filled with the glory of God, as the waters cover the sea' flies in the face of so much that actually happens around us day by day. But while it is important not to become starry-eyed and detached from the suffering of the world, there is a place for the contemplation of the ideal. A hymn such as this provides us with inspiration: this is what the world *should* be like. And when we are aware of this we not only have a glorious vision of what might have been, but we also identify more clearly what is wrong with what is our current state. *Paradise Lost* does exactly this: it contrasts the joyful innocence of the Garden of Eden with the world into which Adam and Eve step hand in hand at the end of the poem. They are the first human beings; they begin a history which takes place outside the protection of a garden. They represent experience and not innocence. But they have known the ideal, and so they can judge how far they have strayed from it. This hymn is like that: it is a kind of *Paradise Lost* in miniature, because it is conscious of sin and grief, of cheerless gloom and pointless life. But it sets against them an ideal which we can have in our hearts, in which the sun is shining and somewhere there is an ideal of a perfect day.

Morning glory, starlit sky
W. H. Vanstone (1923–99)

Morning glory, starlit sky,
  leaves in springtime, swallows' flight,
autumn gales, tremendous seas,
  sounds and scents of summer night;

soaring music, towering words,
  art's perfection, scholar's truth.
joy supreme of human love,
  memory's treasure, grace of youth;

open, Lord, are these, thy gifts,
  gifts of love to mind and sense;
hidden is love's agony,
  love's endeavour, love's expense.

Love that gives, gives ever more,
  gives with zeal, with eager hands,
spares not, keeps not, all outpours,
  ventures all, its all expends.

Drained is love in making full;
  bound in setting others free;
poor in making many rich;
  weak in giving power to be.

Therefore he who thee reveals
  hangs, O Father, on that Tree,
helpless, and the nails and thorns
  tell of what thy love must be.

Thou art God; no monarch thou,
  throned in easy state to reign;
thou art God, whose arms of love
  aching, spent, the world sustain.

This hymn began life as a poem printed at the end of Canon Vanstone's book *Love's Endeavour, Love's Expense* (1977), published in America as *The Risk of Love*. Its sub-title was 'The Response of Being to the Love of God'. It is significant that Vanstone should have ended with a poem: it is almost as if he realized that over a hundred pages of prose were not sufficient to capture the elusive character of the love of God, 'The God Who will not abandon and to Whom nothing save Himself is expendable' (p. 65). There is something about that love that prose, however eloquent, is unable to capture; just as lovers have always written poetry to express their deepest feelings, from Valentine cards to the sonnets of Donne. Something was needed about God's love, and the human response to it, that was beyond the reach of ordinary words. So the book ends with this poem, entitled 'A Hymn to the Creator'.

The hymn begins by listing some of the gifts of God which we enjoy: the beauty of the morning, the stars at night, different weathers and different seasons, all the wonderful variety of nature. It is like the rejoicing of Gerard Manley Hopkins in the sheer difference of things:

> Glory be to God for dappled things –
>> For skies of couple-colour as a brinded cow;
>>> For rose-moles all in stipple upon trout that swim;
>> Fresh fire-coal chestnut-falls; finches' wings;
>>> Landscape plotted and pieced – fold, fallow, and plough . . .
>>>> Praise him.

Then come the gifts of the human mind: music, poetry, painting and sculpture, scholarship and the pursuit of truth. Finally there are the supreme gifts: love, memory, beauty and physical grace. These verses are a catalogue of loveliness: as St Paul said:

> Whatsoever things are true, whatsoever things are honest, whatsoever things are just, whatsoever things are pure, whatsoever things are lovely, whatsoever things are of good report; if there be any virtue, and if there be any praise, think on these things.
>
> (Philippians 4.8)

We can, and should, rejoice in these things. But now the hymn goes deeper, much deeper, because there is another side to love, the 'hidden' side. This is the love which is not for the beautiful and the good, but for others. It is the love which makes demands upon us: in caring for others, in selfless acts, in acts which are costly in terms of our own time and energy, or of our own self-esteem. Love is the opposite of narcissism, that self-love which causes us to admire our own reflection in some spiritual or personal mirror. It is 'love's agony, / love's endeavour, love's expense', the love that tries to do good and that costs something.

When Wordsworth published a poem entitled 'The Idiot Boy', one of his admirers wrote to him saying that this was a poem that could never please. Wordsworth's reply was sternly correct. He said that he had often admired the way in which fathers and mothers looked after their mentally defective children: 'It is there that we see the strength, disinterestedness, and grandeur of love.' He was talking about the human spirit, what in another poem he called 'man's unconquerable mind'. In the same way, this hymn moves from the gifts of perception and sense, through the lovely things of the mind, to a love which is deeper than all those things. It is a love which used to be called 'charity', from the Latin *caritas*, until that word lost its original meaning and became associated with collectors with tins on street corners. Originally 'charity' meant a wide and generous love, an embracing love that went far beyond the simple love of one person for another. It is this love that St Paul speaks of in the wonderful chapter 13 of 1 Corinthians: 'Charity suffereth long, and is kind; charity envieth not; charity vaunteth not itself, is not puffed up . . . and now abideth faith, hope, charity, these three; but the greatest of these is charity.'

In this hymn the love that St Paul speaks of and that the translators of 1611 rendered as 'charity' is described as an outpouring, an eager giving of the self, a love that 'ventures all', that gives everything. But as the next verse makes clear, this love is very demanding. In giving to others, it makes itself poor; in 'making full' it is 'drained'. At this point we begin to see that this love, in human beings, is a reflection of heavenly love. Something which is drained is emptied: it is an echo of the idea that God, in coming to earth, 'emptied himself' of his glory.

The hymn moves subtly and purposefully towards the final vision. Love is exemplified at its fullest in the figure on the cross. This is God, but God helpless. The hymn reiterates the paradoxes at the heart of Christianity: that God, who is love, becomes poor to make others rich; that he becomes weak in order to empower others. Except a grain of wheat fall into the ground and die, it abideth alone; in service is perfect freedom; he that loveth his life shall lose it: all these state the difficult truths which we discover, if we are fortunate, at the centre of the spiritual life.

Christ suffered on the cross, and the nails and thorns tell of his love. His sacrifice is an emblem and an example. As an emblem the figure on the cross reveals God, who is love; as an example, his selfless love is what sustains the world. On the cross his arms ache: but they are also the everlasting arms of love. Even as a helpless victim, the monarch who is now no monarch is engaged in giving himself up to a painful death. This is the central example, the most terrible and wonderful example, of 'love's agony, love's endeavour, love's expense'.

O thou who camest from above
Charles Wesley (1707–88)

O thou who camest from above
  The pure celestial fire to impart,
Kindle a flame of sacred love
  On the mean altar of my heart!

There let it for thy glory burn
  With inextinguishable blaze,
And trembling to its source return,
  In humble prayer and fervent praise.

Jesus, confirm my heart's desire
  To work, and speak, and think for thee;
Still let me guard the holy fire,
  And still stir up thy gift in me;

Ready for all thy perfect will,
  My acts of faith and love repeat,
Till death thy endless mercies seal,
  And make the sacrifice complete.

This hymn has the most unexpected origin. It was written for a collection of hymns, *Short Hymns on Select Passages of the Holy Scriptures*, published in 1762, on a verse that is unlikely ever to be on the list of popular texts, from a book of the Bible that is unlikely ever to be a much-loved book. The 'short hymns' all took their inspiration from individual verses in the Bible, and this one was from Leviticus 6.13: 'The fire shall ever be burning upon the altar; it shall never go out.' Charles Wesley was a genius in his handling of the Bible, here proving that a silk purse *can* be made out of a sow's ear.

The verse comes in the middle of some complicated instructions to Moses about the burnt offering. He had to command Aaron and his sons to make sure that the fire was always burning, and that certain specific offerings were laid upon it. Wesley sees the possibilities of all this: he transforms it by turning the fire on the altar into the inward fire in the human heart. The heart was traditionally seen as the seat of the emotions, and it was used again and again by both Charles Wesley and his brother John. All Methodists know the account which John gave of his 'conversion' on 24 May 1738, in which he said: 'I felt my heart strangely warmed'; and again and again he used the words to refer to the depths of his innermost self. Charles Wesley's hymns, too, are full of references to the heart: 'My heart is full of Christ, and longs / Its glorious matter to declare', or 'My longing heart vouchsafe to make / Thine everlasting throne.'

In the first verse here, 'my heart' comes at the end. It is part of the way in which that verse is very carefully structured, beginning with the Holy Spirit, which came from heaven to impart fire to the disciples; then praying to that spirit – 'kindle a flame of sacred love' – and then leading to 'the mean altar of my heart'. We move from the historical – the first Pentecost – to the particular: 'come to *my* heart'. Already we have left Leviticus far behind: this is now a New Testament hymn, with only a distant glance at the original source in the word 'altar'. And yet the words from Leviticus about the fire, 'it shall never go out', are behind the rest of the hymn. The prayer is that it will burn 'with inextinguishable blaze', that extraordinary word (perhaps the longest word in English hymnody) spectacularly describing the fire going on and on. It is a metaphor for dedication: 'May this fire, now lit in my heart by the Holy Spirit, never go out.' Not surprisingly, therefore, the hymn is often used for ordination or consecration services. It expresses perfectly the continuing, lifelong commitment that a priest undertakes. But it applies to all who would wish to dedicate themselves to Christ.

The fire on the altar flickers and trembles upwards. Charles Wesley imagines a two-way process, in which the Holy Spirit comes down to inspire him, and his response is to give that fire back in prayer and praise. As George Herbert put it, prayer is 'God's breath in man returning to his birth'. The prayer is humble, linking up with the 'mean altar' of verse 1, because Charles Wesley *places* himself beautifully in this hymn: the coming of the Holy Spirit has made him not proud or triumphant, but a person who can pray and praise, an altar for God.

His humanity comes again in verse 3, which takes up the theme of the heart from verse 1. His heart's desire is now 'to work, and speak, and think for thee'. These are all very human things: Charles Wesley has left the world of praise and prayer for the world of action, of doing things – what in the Middle Ages was called the *vita activa* as opposed to the *vita contemplativa*. In the second verse he was worshipping, but now he is acting – working for God, speaking for God, thinking for God. He knows, however, that the original enthusiasm can fade: after all, when he published this hymn in 1762 he had been actively working for the Methodist societies for over 20 years. But his prayer is that he may go on and on working, as long as his strength will last: 'Still let me guard the holy fire.' We are back with the 'inextinguishable blaze' of verse 2, and the altar tended by Aaron and his sons.

The fire needs to be stirred, as fires do: the image is a homely one, but it also comes from 2 Timothy 1.6: 'Stir up the gift of God', which Wesley, as an Anglican priest, would also have known from the Collect for the twenty-fifth Sunday after Trinity, the Sunday Next before Advent: 'Stir up, we beseech thee, O Lord, the wills of thy faithful people . . .' It is a command to begin to think of Advent and Christmas (it used to be said that it was a reminder to stir the Christmas pudding mixture), a command to get ready, to prepare for the birth of Christ. Here the idea of stirring the fire gives rise to stirring up something else – 'the gift in me'. The 'gift', I think, must be the power of the Holy Spirit that he has been celebrating in the first two verses, so that this is a prayer that Jesus may ensure that the gift is continually active.

As the fire leads to 'stir up', so 'stir up' leads to 'ready'. The last verse declares the writer to be prepared to do 'all thy perfect will': he is ready for anything. This again reminds us of George Herbert, who wrote a poem about Aaron; Charles Wesley may well have thought of it when he was writing about Aaron and his sons tending the altar. In 'Aaron', Herbert takes the description of Aaron's clothes (from Exodus 28) and turns it into a metaphor for the 'inner clothing' of a priest:

> Holiness on the head,
> Light and perfections on the breast,
> Harmonious bells below, raising the dead
> To leade them unto life and rest.
> Thus are true Aarons drest.

He reflects that his own sinful self is not like this, but that he can be 'new drest' in Christ, so that he is worthy (though not through his own worthiness) to be a parish priest. At the end of the poem he is ready: 'Come people: Aaron's drest.'

Something like this is implied in Charles Wesley's 'ready' (and in another hymn he used the phrase 'clothed in righteousness divine'). But his readiness is not to receive the people at the Holy Communion, as Herbert's is, but for a life of service: 'My acts of faith and love repeat'. The pattern suggested by 'repeat' is of day after day, month after month, year after year, devoted to acts of Christian duty: this is no sudden or temporary irruption of the Holy Spirit into his life, but a continuous process, keeping the altar fire going until the end. It is an echo of the prayer attributed to Sir Francis Drake:

> O Lord God, when thou givest to thy servants to endeavour any great matter, grant us to know that it is not the beginning, but the continuing of the same unto the end, until it be thoroughly finished, which yieldeth the true glory.

Here the prayer is to continue the acts of faith and love for the remainder of life. The only thing that should conclude this daily repeating of those acts is death itself.

And death is the crowning mercy, the final act that concludes all the other mercies – the fire in the heart, the sacred love, the inextinguishable blaze, the working, speaking and thinking for Christ. These are the stuff of the Christian life, lived to the uttermost stretch of human ability through the inspiration of the Holy Spirit. They are God's 'endless mercies', in response to which the fire is kept going on the altar of the heart, until the end of life, when the sacrifice ceases and the life is complete. The word 'sacrifice' takes us back to the origins of the poem in the chapter from Leviticus. It is another word for the process of daily living inspired by the Holy Spirit, and continuing to the end until, with death, the pattern of a Christian life is revealed in its entirety, a completed pattern of faith and love.

GOD'S WORLD: PILGRIMAGE AND THANKFULNESS

Who would true valour see
John Bunyan (1628–88)

Who would true valour see,
  Let him come hither;
One here will constant be,
  Come wind, come weather.
There's no discouragement
Shall make him once relent
His first avowed intent
  To be a pilgrim.

Whoso beset him round
  With dismal stories,
Do but themselves confound,
  His strength the more is.
No lion can him fright,
He'll with a giant fight,
But he will have a right
  To be a pilgrim.

Hobgoblin, nor foul fiend,
  Can daunt his spirit:
He knows he at the end
  Shall life inherit.
Then, fancies, fly away,
He'll fear not what men say,
He'll labour night and day
  To be a pilgrim.

John Bunyan was a great preacher and writer, and a hero of the
nonconformist tradition. He was born into a family that had seen
better days: he himself was a travelling tinker, mending pots and
pans in the towns and villages around Bedford. He was a strong
character, a courageous man who served in the Parliamentary

army under General Fairfax during the Civil War, and who later refused to stop preaching when ordered to do so by the magistrates under the laws brought in at the Restoration. He spent long years in prison for his defiance. His rough, strong, stubborn character is beautifully summed up by Rudyard Kipling in his poem 'The Holy War':

A tinker out of Bedford,
  A vagrant oft in quod,
A private under Fairfax,
  A minister of God.

His greatest achievement was *The Pilgrim's Progress*, from which this song is taken. It comes from Part II, published in 1684, where it is sung by Mr Valiant-for-Truth, who has been fighting those who would try to stop him living the Christian life. The pilgrims meet him 'with his sword drawn, and his face all bloody': he had been fighting three men, Wildhead, Inconsiderate and Pragmatick, and won the victory over them and over others who would have discouraged him.

It was not used in a hymn book until 200 years later, and only became well known when Ralph Vaughan Williams found a folk tune to fit it. That tune was printed in the *English Hymnal* of 1906, but to words which were different. The words, beginning 'He who would valiant be', were by Percy Dearmer, who thought Bunyan's language too quaint and old-fashioned, and produced an early twentieth-century version that imitated Bunyan and at times followed him. Since that time, the two texts have existed side by side, often in the same book, both set to the same tune.

The Pilgrim's Progress is a great classic of evangelical literature because it is built on the idea of a journey, a journey 'from this world to that which is to come', as the title page says. In Part I Christian meets many adventures, hardships and discouragements before he finally crosses the river to the holy city. In Part II his wife Christiana and her children follow in his footsteps with the help of Mr Greatheart, the pastor and guide, and it is during their journey that they meet Mr Valiant-for-Truth.

The idea of a pilgrimage is a very ancient one. It occurs in many religions, and stands for something very important – the leaving of home and comfort, and the setting out towards some holy place. It requires an effort of will to start, to go forth and leave the familiar; it requires perseverance to travel on to the end of the road; it brings with it the satisfaction of having somehow come closer to the reality of the holy by journeying to some sacred place. So pilgrims journey to Mecca, or to Varanasi, or to Rome. In the Middle Ages it was common to make pilgrimages to Canterbury to the shrine of St Thomas, or to Santiago de Compostella to the shrine of St James, and some of these pilgrimages are still of great significance. They allow people to satisfy something deep within themselves: the need to search for the sacred.

At the same time pilgrimage is also a metaphor. It is one of the most powerful of all representations of how we interpret and understand life itself: that we are on a journey from birth to death, during which we will meet with many adventures; we travel on, uphill and downhill, sometimes across deserts and sometimes in beautiful places. Bunyan's hymn, old-fashioned though it may sound, represents something that lies deep within all of us. It is easy, for example, to be blown off course, or to give up: but the first verse says 'One here will constant be' and that nothing will discourage the 'first avowed intent / To be a pilgrim'. Sometimes people try to frighten pilgrims with the stories of the troubles ahead, but the true pilgrim will go on and on. His Christian perseverance in the right way, undeterred and unfrightened, will give him the right to call himself a true pilgrim; and he will press on to the end, undaunted by fiends or devils and caring nothing for the opinions of the people around him.

The hymn is about the pilgrimage of life for everyone. But we can also read back into these lines Bunyan's own determination, his refusal to give in to demands that he should stop preaching, his acceptance of long years in prison, his indifference to popular opinion. In the end, his steadfastness made him something of a hero in his own time, but that was after years of suffering. He refused to give up: and all the time he was writing books which have become famous in the catalogue of Puritan experience literature – *Grace Abounding to the Chief of Sinners*, *The Holy War*, *The Pilgrim's Progress*. His persistence can be seen in every line of the hymn, in the way in which the violent and strange rhymes of the first part of each verse – 'hither / weather', 'stories / more is', 'spirit / inherit' – seem to be beaten out on some anvil of language:

they suggest effort and struggle. And then, in the second half of each verse, the rhymes come in threes, more easily, leading up each time to the one unrhymed word which is the climax of every verse – 'pilgrim'. Each verse seems to be another step along the way: 'pilgrim', 'pilgrim', 'pilgrim'. The hymn is a wonderful example of the joy, as well as the hardship, of what it is like 'to be a pilgrim'.

And the reward is something that is denied to those who never set out on the journey. It is easy to stay at home, spiritually, and never question the way in which life is being lived. It is not a question of going to church, or adhering to a faith; it is a question of living life as a journey of the spirit, of recognizing one's limitations and trying to overcome them. Bunyan's Christian goes through all the problems that a pilgrimage entails – the slough of despond, the valley of humiliation, the hill difficulty, vanity fair, doubting castle, and many more. They are emblems of what all people feel who are not content with sitting back and enjoying life. But at the end the pilgrims, Christian and Hopeful, enter the city, and are transfigured, and 'had raiment put on that shone like gold'. And when Mr Valiant-for-Truth came to the river of death, 'He passed over, and all the trumpets sounded for him on the other side.'

Guide me, O thou great Jehovah

William Williams (1717–91), translated by Peter Williams (1722–96) and others

Guide me, O thou great Jehovah,
  Pilgrim through this barren land;
I am weak, but thou art mighty,
  Hold me with thy powerful hand:
    Bread of heaven,
    Feed me till I want no more.

Open thou the crystal fountain,
  Whence the healing stream doth flow;
Let the fire and cloudy pillar
  Lead me all my journey through:
    Strong Deliverer,
    Be thou still my strength and shield.

When I tread the verge of Jordan,
  Bid my anxious fears subside;
Death of death, and hell's destruction,
  Land me safe on Canaan's side:
    Songs of praises
    I will ever give to thee.

The narrative of the escape of the children of Israel from the land of Egypt is one of the great stories of the world. It begins with their slavery, and the promise to Moses in the encounter with the burning bush (Exodus 3). It continues with Moses saying to Pharaoh, again and again, 'Let my people go', while plague after plague tormented the Egyptians; until after the killing of all the first-born of Egypt, Pharaoh finally yielded (Exodus 12.31), and the Israelites left, passing through the Red Sea in which all of

Pharaoh's pursuing cavalry were drowned. During their journey through the desert they were guided by a pillar of cloud by day and a pillar of fire by night (Exodus 13.21); but they met with many hardships, and often complained. They had no food, but God sent them manna (Exodus 16); and no water, until God told Moses to strike the rock, and water came out (Exodus 17). Finally, after many adventures and long wandering in the desert, they crossed the river Jordan and came to the promised land of Canaan, a land flowing with milk and honey.

This pilgrimage through the wilderness to freedom has become an inspiration to writers and political leaders for centuries. Martin Luther King, Jr, who led the civil rights movement in America in the 1960s, was a second Moses, leading his people towards equality and fair treatment. His death in 1968 meant that, like Moses, he saw the promised land from afar but did not live to cross over into it: but throughout his life, the civil rights movement drew on the African–American slave songs which had their origins in the Bible:

> When Israel was in Egypt's land:
>   Let my people go,
> Oppressed so hard they could not stand,
>   Let my people go.
>
> Go down, Moses,
>   Way down in Egypt land,
> Tell old Pharaoh,
>   Let my people go.

The appalling cruelties of the slave system reproduced the conditions of the Israelites long ago, who groaned under the bondage in Egypt and were freed with the help of God. And Martin Luther King's famous 'I have a dream' speech at the march on Washington in August 1963 ended with the words of the old spiritual: 'Free at last. Free at last. Thank God Almighty, we're free at last.'

But the Exodus story, like all good stories, works at another level. The journey of the children of Israel through the desert is an emblem of life itself, the pilgrimage through the barren land before the crossing of the Jordan into the promised land of heaven. The various episodes are pressed into service to show the working of divine providence: the bread of heaven, the crystal fountain, the fire and cloudy pillar. These are emblems of the care and love of God. He 'feeds' us, gives us 'the healing stream', and guides us on the way. At the end of that journey we come to the river of Jordan: we pray that our fear of death may be taken away, and that after crossing the river of death we may be kindly judged and land safe in heaven, where we will sing the praises of God for ever and ever. But human fears are natural, and the 'anxious fears' are there, as they were for Christian at the end of *The Pilgrim's Progress*. He feels that he is going to drown, but Hopeful says, 'Be of good cheer, my brother, I feel the bottom, and it is good.' The scene that follows is very dramatic, as Christian struggles in the water; but Hopeful says:

> Be of good cheer, Jesus Christ maketh thee whole: and with that, Christian brake out with a loud voice, Oh I see him again! And he tells me, When thou passest through the waters I will be with thee, and through the rivers, they shall not overflow thee. Then they both took courage, and the enemy was after that as still as a stone, until they were gone over. Christian therefore presently found ground to stand upon; and so it followed that the rest of the river was but shallow.

The hymn is therefore concerned with the broad patterns of life: the pilgrimage, God's providence, death and judgement ('Land me safe on Canaan's side'). But the phrase 'Strong Deliverer' points to yet another level of meaning. This springs from the New Testament rather than from the Old Testament. If we read 'Strong Deliverer' as Jesus Christ, then the three verses become a hymn about freedom from sin. *Hymns Ancient and Modern* and the *English Hymnal* certainly wanted to emphasize this interpretation, for they both changed the first line to 'Guide me, O thou great Redeemer'.

In this reading the journey of the children of Israel from slavery in Egypt to freedom in Canaan is what used to be called a 'type': an episode in the Old Testament that prefigures something that is revealed in the New Testament. A typological reading of the episode of Moses striking the rock to provide water was given by St Paul in 1 Corinthians 10.4: 'For they drank of that spiritual Rock that followed them: and that Rock was Christ.' In this reading of the journey through the barren land, they all ate the same spiritual meat, and all drank the same spiritual drink. The freedom from bondage becomes the freedom from sin, and the bread of heaven is Jesus, the bread of life (John 6.31–51); the water of life is the 'living water' promised to the woman of Samaria (John 4.10–14). A nineteenth-century hymn puts it with beautiful simplicity:

> I hunger and I thirst;
>   Jesus, my manna be:
> Ye living waters, burst
>   Out of the rock for me . . .
>
> Rough paths my feet have trod
>   Since first their course began;
> Feed me, thou Bread of God;
>   Help me, thou Son of Man.
>
> For still the desert lies
>   My thirsting soul before;
> O living waters, rise
>   Within me evermore.

The freedom from being a slave to sin, and the experience of the glorious liberty of the children of God, are classic ways for expressing the joy of salvation. Charles Wesley uses them often:

> Captain of Israel's host and Guide
>   Of all who seek the land above,
> Beneath thy shadow we abide,
>   The cloud of thy protecting love . . .
>
> By thine unerring Spirit led,
>   We shall not in the desert stray . . .

William Williams's hymn, therefore, expresses our longings and hopes in different ways. It draws on the wonderful Exodus story, with an emphasis on God's providential care through life and into death; but it also presents a type or emblem of the saving love of God in Jesus Christ. Through that love we are conducted out of bondage; in bonds of sin, imprisoned in our own selfishness, we march slowly and with great difficulty through the desert, trying to find the promised land. As Charles Wesley wrote, very beautifully, in another hymn:

> O that I now, from sin released,
>   Thy word may to the utmost prove,
> Enter into the promised rest,
>   The Canaan of thy perfect love.

Lead, kindly Light
John Henry Newman (1801–90)

Lead, kindly Light, amid the encircling gloom,
    Lead thou me on:
The night is dark, and I am far from home,
    Lead thou me on.
Keep thou my feet; I do not ask to see
The distant scene; one step enough for me.

I was not ever thus, nor prayed that thou
    Should'st lead me on;
I loved to choose and see my path; but now
    Lead thou me on.
I loved the garish day, and, spite of fears,
Pride ruled my will: remember not past years.

So long thy power hath blest me, sure it still
    Will lead me on,
O'er moor and fen, o'er crag and torrent, till
    The night is gone,
And with the morn those angel faces smile,
Which I have loved long since, and lost awhile.

In December 1832, a young Oxford don set out with two friends on a tour of Italy. John Henry Newman, Fellow of Oriel College and already an expert on the Fathers of the early Church, was accompanied by his friend Hurrell Froude and Froude's father. Hurrell Froude went in search of health, and Newman had been overworking. They went by boat from Falmouth, calling at various Mediterranean ports such as Corfu and Malta on the way. They visited Sicily and Naples, reaching Rome in March 1833. It seems to have been a cultural rather than a religious tour: Newman was a clergyman of the Church of England, much concerned about the state of the Church but in no way, at this time, inclined towards

Roman Catholicism. However, when the Froudes left Rome in April 1833 to travel back to England by land, he decided to stay longer, and went back to Naples and then to Sicily for a second look.

In Sicily he fell ill. He was desperately sick, probably with typhoid fever, in a remote village, where he lay for three weeks. Feeling somewhat better, he was helped to Palermo, where he hoped to get a boat to take him to Marseilles and thence home. But there was no boat available, and he had to wait for three more weeks before finding a berth in an orange boat, which was then becalmed for yet another week in the Straits of Bonifacio, between Corsica and Sardinia. It was there that Newman wrote 'Lead, kindly Light'.

It is hard for us to imagine the difficulties of travel in 1833. Today, in Newman's situation, we would book a seat on the first plane back as soon as we were fit enough to travel. He had to get better, and then wait, and then take a cargo boat, and finally spend a whole week at sea hoping for a wind. He took to writing poems during these long days, and 'Lead, kindly Light' was one of them, written on 16 June. He was still weak from his illness; he was also unquiet in his mind. In his own words, 'The strangeness of foreign life threw me back into myself.' Before he left Oxford, and during the journey when he had news from friends, he was worried about the state of the Church of England. He thought that it was weak and lethargic, and that it was subject to all kinds of pressure from a reforming government. As he put it 30 years later, in his autobiographical *Apologia Pro Vita Sua* (1864):

> The Whigs had come into power; Lord Grey had told the Bishops to set their house in order, and some of the Prelates had been insulted and threatened in the streets of London. The vital question was how were we to keep the Church from being liberalized?

Behind this anxiety was the whole question of the government of the Church of England. Newman was worried that the Liberal government would interfere with the running of the Church, as indeed it did. There was strong anti-clerical feeling abroad, and many of the bishops had made matters worse by voting against the Reform Bill in 1832, which was why they were shouted at and insulted in the street. Newman was keen to get back home to play a part in opposing what he saw as a danger to the Church, and when he did arrive he was one of the foremost figures in what became known as the 'Oxford Movement', stressing the Church as a divine institution with an authority depending on the apostolic succession.

We have to imagine him, therefore, stuck in the middle of the Mediterranean, gradually convalescing from a dangerous illness, and beset by problems and anxieties about what he would be faced with when he arrived home. It was then that he began to write:

> Lead, kindly Light, amid the encircling gloom,
>   Lead Thou me on;
> The night is dark, and I am far from home,
>   Lead Thou me on.
> Keep Thou my feet; I do not ask to see
> The distant scene; one step enough for me.

The reader instantly imagines a wanderer in the darkness, far from home, following a light that is 'kindly', the only thing that is helpful. The long lines followed by the short ones suggest a movement that is quick and then slow, stopping at the end of the second and fourth lines: the verse seems to stumble along, like a traveller trying to find the way in the dark. Newman said in the *Apologia* that during these years he felt 'that my mind had not found its ultimate rest, and that in some sense or other I was on journey'. He was, he thought, 'slowly advancing ... and led on by God's hand blindly, not knowing whither He is taking me'.

In the dark, one of the most difficult things for a walker is to know where to place his feet. Even if he has a light as a guide, every step is a problem – mud, or marsh, or tussock, or rock. So Newman asks God to 'keep his feet', to make sure that each step is safe and right. There are echoes of many parts of the Bible in the word 'keep': the song of Hannah in 1 Samuel 2 says 'He will keep the feet of his saints' (verse 9). The word has many meanings: to hold fast ('O keep my soul'), to protect ('The Lord bless thee and keep thee'), to preserve ('He shall give his angels charge over thee, to keep thee'), to observe ('If ye love me, keep my commandments'). So when Newman says 'Keep thou my feet', he is, perhaps unconsciously, drawing on all these meanings. And it is enough if he can go on, step by step, stumbling through the darkness: one step at a time is all that he prays for.

As a metaphor for the human condition, this is an extremely powerful verse: it gives a picture of this figure in the dark, trying to find where to go. Then the second verse reflects on his situation. Like other travellers before him, the poet looks back at a time when he was 'careless'. In broad daylight it was easy to choose a path, and he did not bother with God. Thinking about serious things was not important then: there were plenty of other things to think about, plenty to distract him from the reality that he did not know his way and he was stumbling about in the darkness of life. He was proud, and 'loved the garish day', in ways that now make him ashamed ('Remember not past years').

And so the third verse turns away from this remembrance to a trust that God will bring him through the darkness to the morning. The landscape is wild that he will have to cross – 'moor and fen . . . crag and torrent' – but he thinks he can cross it through the night until the daybreak comes and he can see his way safely again. And when that comes, when the night is gone

> And with the morn those angel faces smile,
> Which I have loved long since, and lost awhile.

This is a magical moment, as the daylight brings back to him not just a pathway, but the faces of those he had known and lost. Who are they? Nobody knows, and Newman quite rightly resisted any attempt to explain them. They may refer to the friends he had left at home, before setting out on his voyage; or to a vision of angels as a sign of heaven. He had lost the earthly friends or the angel faces, alone on a becalmed ship, not sure where he was going, 'all at sea' we might say. Newman's friend Charles Marriott thought that these lines 'touched on the idea that infants have a more intimate communion with the unseen world', and certainly children in the nineteenth century were often thought of as 'little angels'; they were carved on tombstones and painted in the margins of books as angels with the faces of little children. If this is the meaning, it points towards a time of childhood, and suggests that Newman was longing to come through the dark night of the soul to a morning that would be one of the simple innocence that he had known.

Everyone longs for a solution to the problems of life which will bring back some lost ideal world, a world of light, and sunshine, and children's voices, before the complexities of adult life set in. Newman's hymn faces up to the darkness of the soul as his traveller stumbles through the darkness; he then remembers the superficial good times, and is ashamed of them; and in the third verse he holds out a hope that one day, somehow, he will come out of the darkness into a blessed light, in which he sees the faces of loved ones, and they smile to him. Those smiles are deeply touching: they must have brought comfort to many who have lost children, and who have a vision that one day they will come out of the darkness of loss and bereavement to meet those faces again, smiling gently in the welcome of heaven. And who is to say that they are wrong to think like this? We should treasure such crumbs of hope as we stumble through our own times of difficulty, not knowing where we are going, struggling over crag and through torrent. To have something to hope for at the end is a powerful incentive to keep going; one day, somehow, we hope to see the faces of those whom we loved, and have lost, and we hope to see them smile in peace and joy.

Now thank we all our God
Martin Rinkart (1586–1649), translated by Catherine Winkworth (1827–78)

———◆———

Now thank we all our God,
  With hearts and hands and voices,
Who wondrous things hath done,
  In whom his world rejoices;
Who from our mothers' arms
  Hath blessed us on our way
With countless gifts of love,
  And still is ours to-day.

Oh may this bounteous God
  Through all our life be near us,
With ever joyful hearts
  And blessed peace to cheer us;
And keep us in his grace,
  And guide us when perplexed,
And free us from all ills
  In this world and the next.

All praise and thanks to God
  The Father, now be given,
The Son, and Him who reigns
  With them in highest heaven,
The One eternal God,
  Whom earth and heaven adore,
For thus it was, is now,
  And shall be evermore!

This grand and simple hymn was translated by Catherine Winkworth from the German of Martin Rinkart or Rinckart, who was the Lutheran pastor in the town of Eilenburg near Leipzig in Saxony from 1617 to 1649. Those were the years of what is called the Thirty Years' War (1618–48), a period of great suffering and unhappiness for the people of the German states and principalities, as the warring armies, Protestant and Catholic, marched through Europe creating havoc and destruction wherever they went (Berthold Brecht's play *Mother Courage* is based on this period). Eilenburg was a walled town, which attracted refugees from the surrounding countryside; it became hopelessly overcrowded, and suffered from food shortages and disease. During a particularly severe epidemic of the plague in 1637, Rinkart was the only pastor in the town, and he is said to have officiated at more than 40 funerals in one day at the height of the plague. One of the victims was his wife. At one time he is said to have saved the town of Eilenburg from the depredations of a detachment of the Swedish army by the singing of a famous Reformation hymn by Paul Eber (1511–69), '*Wenn wir in höchsten Nöthen sein*' ('When we are in the greatest trouble'). The Swedish commander had demanded the sum of £4,500 from the inhabitants, but was so moved by the singing that he accepted the much smaller sum of 2,000 florins.

So if Brecht portrayed a Mother Courage, we may think of Rinkart as a Father Courage, the devoted pastor among his people, never deserting them and keeping up their spirits in defiance of their sufferings and his own bereavement. His great hymn is not just one of thankfulness but of bravery, because it takes bravery to write such a hymn of trust in God when the circumstances are so awful. It is easy to trust in God when life is rich and fulfilled; but to those who endured year after year of war and pestilence, it must have been very difficult to believe in the goodness of God. Rinkart must have had a childlike faith and a deep devotion to write as he did.

It is a very grand hymn, sometimes known as the German *Te Deum*, a hymn for great occasions and notable festivals. This is partly because it has a magnificent tune, well suited to large congregations and great buildings. But it seems to have started life as a much more ordinary hymn, and it is good to think of it as simple as well as grand. In one of the earliest published texts it is entitled '*Tisch-Gebetlein*' ('A little prayer at table'), which suggests a grace before a meal. If we think of it in this way, we can visualize

Rinkart and his family saying or singing the hymn daily, even in times of starvation and hardship. Every day they would reaffirm their belief in the goodness of God, in spite of all the stress of the political and social world outside. That takes not only courage but perseverance and the ability to endure hardship, like a good soldier of Christ.

The first two verses are based on Ecclesiasticus 50.22–4:

> Now therefore bless ye the God of all, which only doeth wondrous things every where, which exalteth our days from the womb, and dealeth with us according to his mercy.
> He grant us joyfulness of heart, and that peace may be in our days in Israel for ever:
> That he would confirm his mercy with us, and deliver us at his time!

The third verse of the hymn is a paraphrase of the *Gloria Patri* ('Glory be to the Father, and to the Son, and to the Holy Ghost . . .').

The verses from Ecclesiasticus have a timeless quality, but they also have an application to Rinkart's own time. The prayer for 'blessed peace to cheer us' would have been felt with particular intensity during the Thirty Years' War, and so would the prayer to 'free us from all ills / In this world and the next'. At the same time the gratitude to God as 'this bounteous God' would have been a remarkable testimony of faith in an age when starvation and disease were all around. There is something heroic in this defiance of circumstances: it is the heroism of Job – 'Though he slay me, yet will I trust him' (13.15) – and the defiance is that of the truly noble man. That man does not grumble, or curse his fate: he gets on with life, as Rinkart did, accepting his lot and doing his best. And at this point thankfulness, which is the central message of the hymn, becomes not only a sublime quality, but also an indication of character.

The beauty of Rinkart's hymn is in its complete and unwavering trust. We have to think of him as the humble pastor, never doubting, but giving thanks; and in that giving of thanks he becomes a model of the Christian who is content with what he has, and is free from envy and covetousness. It is very easy to feel discontented because other people have easier lives, or more worldly goods, or more dashing lifestyles; but there is something very simple and touching in the very act of thankfulness itself. In praying the very words of the General Thanksgiving we become better men and women, because as we do so we realize that we are indeed fortunate to be alive:

> Almighty God, Father of all mercies, we thine unworthy servants do give thee most humble and hearty thanks for all thy goodness and loving-kindness to us, and to all men; We bless thee for our creation, preservation, and all the blessings of this life; but above all, for thine inestimable love in the redemption of the world by our Lord Jesus Christ; for the means of grace, and for the hope of glory.

The prayer reminds us of life itself, and our enjoyment of it. But it goes much further. It reminds us of our own unworthiness, and of the redemption of the world undertaken for us. However unworthy we are, we are loved by God; just as we are accepted for what we are by others, and loved by them, in a human replication of divine love.

It is not surprising that Rinkart's hymn is found all over the world; for in the very act of thankfulness we understand ourselves better, and reveal the best side of our human nature. However imperfect and unworthy we may be at other times, we achieve something like nobility and self-understanding in thanking God; and if we continue to do so in times of suffering and bereavement we become, like Rinkart, heroic.

For the beauty of the earth
Folliott Sandford Pierpoint
(1835–1917)

For the beauty of the earth,
 For the beauty of the skies,
For the love which from our birth
 Over and around us lies:
 Christ our God, to thee we raise
 This our sacrifice of praise.

For the beauty of each hour
 Of the day and of the night,
Hill and vale, and tree and flower,
 Sun and moon and stars of light:

For the joy of ear and eye,
 For the heart and brain's delight,
For the mystic harmony
 Linking sense to sound and sight:

For the joy of human love,
 Brother, sister, parent, child,
Friends on earth, and friends above,
 For all gentle thoughts and mild:

For each perfect gift of thine
 To our race so freely given,
Graces human and divine,
 Flowers of earth and buds of heaven:
 Christ our God, to thee we raise
 This our sacrifice of praise.

This is a hymn of thanksgiving. It is good for us to give thanks at all times, and not only in prosperous and happy ones. My grandfather used to sing, 'Count your blessings, name them one by one

/ And it will surprise you what the Lord hath done.' And in both good times and bad, this hymn can recall us to a sense of gratitude for the simple things of life, such as the beauty of nature. We need not wait for the spectacular moments. As Wordsworth put it, if we look for blessings, we can find them to be 'A simple produce of the common day'.

It is the words 'simple' and 'common' that are important here. Wordsworth is reminding us of the joy of ordinary things, and this hymn does the same. It begins with the plainest line, 'For the beauty of the earth' and goes on to repeat that with the beauty of the skies in the second line. These are the broadest and grandest things, earth and skies, and both can be very lovely. Just how lovely is shown in the second verse, where we read of the beauty of landscape, 'hill and vale, and tree and flower', and remember the wonder of the sun and moon and stars. Every hour of the day and the night has its different beauties, and this hymn celebrates them all.

There are other things to be thankful for too: painting and music, and the gifts of eyes to see and ears to hear. There is a 'mystic harmony' that allows us to see a painting and interpret it, or hear music and understand it, as our brains link 'sense' to sound and sight; it is as though the hymn is describing a process of relationship between ourselves and the outer world, the intricate workings of a nervous system that permits us to see and make sense of the external world. This is 'the heart and brain's delight': the world outside us appeals to our minds, but also to our emotions and feelings. We can find out about the sun, moon and stars scientifically, and we can admire them too, and feel their beauty in our hearts. Indeed, William Blake thought that it was a great mistake to be limited to one way of seeing these things, to what he called 'single vision'. He posed a question in one of his 'Prophetic Books':

> 'What', it will be questioned, 'when the sun rises, do you not see a round disk of fire somewhat like a guinea?' 'Oh no, no, I see an innumerable company of the heavenly host crying "Holy, holy, holy, is the Lord God Almighty".'

Blake was affirming the right of the human mind to hold two things (or more) in the mind at the same time – the scientific knowledge of the sun, and the feeling that its splendour shows forth the glory of God. This hymn does the same thing, though slightly differently. The first three verses speak of beauty, love and joy, and each verse then relates that to Christ our God – to God the Creator, whom we know through his incarnate self as Jesus Christ. The beauty that we sing about – hill and vale, and tree and flower – is the beauty for which we give thanks to the God who made it. And because that God is Christ, we acknowledge in passing that God the Creator is also God the Redeemer.

The hymn is in fact more complicated than it looks. At first it seems as if it is a straightforward celebration of the beauty of the world and the blessings of life. But it goes on to speak of other things, especially of love and friendship: of 'the joy of human love', the love of parents and children, the love of friends. These friends are not only the friends whom we know and love on earth: they are those we have loved who have died. We are giving thanks, as the hymn says, 'for those we love within the veil'. As we do so, we catch a glimpse of something more than the beauty of the earth: we affirm a belief in another life beyond this, in which love and friendship somehow survive death. We all know the feeling, when someone whom we love dies, that the relationship does not end there; we go on loving them, cherishing the memory, revisiting the past, enriching our lives with the affection and respect that we had for them. These can be the 'gentle thoughts and mild' that fill our hearts, and which we can be thankful for; although we can and should be thankful for *all* our good and kind thoughts – what Wordsworth, in another poem, called 'Those little, nameless, unremembered acts / Of kindness and of love'.

Gradually the hymn is moving away from the beauty of the earth as its main theme. It is moving towards a whole view of human life, in which we give thanks for that beauty but also recognize the way in which it fits into a whole scheme of things, in which the beauty of earth is only part of the picture. That picture includes the sense that human love is as precious as natural beauty, and the belief that this earth must be seen in relation to heaven. The gifts of God in Christ, freely given, are heavenly gifts. Seen in us, they are gifts that are human and divine. We can all see the glory of God in human beings and their actions (just as we can see the opposite in the wickedness of human actions). But good actions allow us to perceive the divine in the human. Every good person, in Gerard Manley Hopkins's poem, 'acts in God's eye what in God's eye he is / Christ':

> For Christ plays in ten thousand places,
> Lovely in limbs, and lovely in eyes not his
> To the Father through the features of men's faces.

This hymn puts it slightly differently but very strikingly: the flowers on earth are the buds of heaven. Normally the bud would come before the flowers, but in this reading the flowers of earth – the good lives – are the preparations for a new and better flowering in heaven. These are the perfect gifts – the human graces that prepare us for heaven; and they do so because of the divine gifts – our Lord Jesus Christ, the means of grace, and the promise of heaven, the hope of glory. The ideas are packed into the last two lines to give a very touching sense of what Isaac Watts once called, in the title of one of his hymns, 'heavenly joy on earth'; and this hymn suggests that we can live such lives on earth that we can also have the opposite, earthly joys in heaven: beauty, love, joy.

The hymn has yet one more twist of meaning. The refrain to each verse ends 'this our sacrifice of praise'. It is an echo of the thanksgiving prayer after Holy Communion: 'We thy humble servants entirely desire thy fatherly goodness mercifully to accept this our sacrifice of praise and thanksgiving.' All the thankfulness of the hymn, and all the hopes of heaven, are gathered up into a moment in the service in which the partaker has experienced the forgiving love of Jesus Christ; for the service of Holy Communion includes our sinfulness, the remembrance of things past which 'is grievous unto us', and then moves through the 'comfortable words' of Jesus to the sharing of the bread and wine. Those comfortable words remind us that we are loved and forgiven:

> Come unto me all that travail and are heavy laden, and I will refresh you . . . God so loved the world, that he gave his only-begotten Son, to the end that all that believe in him should not perish, but have everlasting life.

At that moment, in all our unworthiness, we are accepted and allowed to break bread and drink wine at his table. It is one of the moments in which all our earthly humanity is transformed, a moment of beauty and loveliness that calls forth all our thankfulness and love.

Pierpoint, a Victorian schoolmaster and man of letters who lived on into the early twentieth century, wrote three more verses (all eight are printed in the *English Hymnal*). But the present five-verse text makes a very appropriate shortening, because the hymn, which begins with the beauty of the earth, ends with the same beauty. But that beauty is not just the beauty of nature: it is the beauty of our best selves, transfigured and redeemed, still on earth but made ready for heaven. And it calls forth all our thankfulness, not only for the gifts of beauty and love on this earth, but for the whole state of ourselves as redeemed human beings, so that we do indeed find ourselves engaged in a joyful sacrifice of praise.

GOD'S PEOPLE: PRAYER
AND DEDICATION

Prayer is the soul's sincere desire
James Montgomery (1771–1854)

Prayer is the soul's sincere desire,
    Uttered or unexpressed;
The motion of a hidden fire,
    That trembles in the breast.

Prayer is the burden of a sigh,
    The falling of a tear,
The upward glancing of an eye,
    When none but God is near.

Prayer is the simplest form of speech
    That infant lips can try,
Prayer the sublimest strains that reach
    The majesty on high.

Prayer is the contrite sinner's voice,
    Returning from his ways;
While angels in their songs rejoice,
    And cry, 'Behold, he prays!'

Prayer is the Christian's vital breath,
    The Christian's native air,
His watchword at the gates of death:
    He enters heaven with prayer.

In prayer on earth the saints are one,
    In word, and deed, and mind,
When with the Father and his Son
    Sweet fellowship they find.

Nor prayer is made on earth alone;
    The Holy Spirit pleads,
And Jesus, on the eternal throne,
    For sinners intercedes.

> O Thou, by whom we come to God,
>   The Life, the Truth, the Way,
> The path of prayer Thyself hast trod:
>   Lord, teach us how to pray!

Prayer is not an easy business. John Donne, Dean of St Paul's in the early seventeenth century, summed up the problems that many people feel:

> I throw myself down in my chamber, and I call in, and invite God, and his angels thither, and when they are there I neglect God and his angels, for the noise of a fly, for the rattling of a coach, for the whining of a door; I talk on, in the same posture of praying; eyes lifted up; knees bowed down; as though I prayed to God; and if God or his angels should ask me, when I thought last about God in that prayer, I cannot tell: sometimes I forget what I was about, but when I began to forget it, I cannot tell.

This hymn is kind to those of us who find that, like Donne, our attention is easily distracted by any little thing, or our minds are prone to wander. We all need help and reassurance that, even in *trying* to pray, we may be doing right. And prayer is more than just words: according to Montgomery, it is the 'sincere desire' of the human soul, whether it is expressed in words or not. It can be 'the motion of a *hidden* fire', something deep inside us that is never seen by others, but which trembles in our inmost hearts.

One of the disciples, perhaps speaking for them all, acknowledged the difficulty of praying when he said to Jesus, 'Lord, teach us to pray' (Luke 11.1). The request indicates that they guessed that prayer was somehow important, but did not quite know how to go about it. Jesus' response was to teach them what we now call 'The Lord's Prayer', that wonderfully complex, compressed and beautiful prayer that takes in so much that is important: praying for the coming of the kingdom of God in the world; praying for our material needs, such as daily bread, and for our spiritual needs, such as forgiveness and being spared temptation; and glorifying God. It is a prayer that surpasses all others, not only because it came from Jesus himself, but also because it touches our world and ourselves so deeply: it penetrates to the heart of our human need and holds up for us a human ideal.

Montgomery's hymn does not tell us how to pray (he wrote another hymn, 'Lord, teach us how to pray aright', which does that). This hymn is much more concerned with the kind of thing that prayer is. As the first verse tells us, it can be silent prayer, something coming from deep within us; or it can be the burden of a sigh, or the falling of a tear. It can speak to our sadness, as it does when we encounter the death of someone we love, or when we are in despair about something; or it can be a looking upwards towards God, what Montgomery beautifully describes as 'the upward glancing of an eye', as if a quick glance is all we dare to risk in the presence of God.

It can be sad, or tentatively hopeful. It can also be both simple and sublime, as verse 3 tells us. Prayer comes from the lips of innocent children, praying to be good in the only language that they know; and prayer comes from the greatest utterances of the human spirit. Handel's *Messiah* is a sublime prayer, as he acknowledged when he said that 'I did think I did see all Heaven before me, and the great God himself'. So is Beethoven's *Missa Solemnis* and Brahms's *German Requiem*, and Milton's *Paradise Lost* and all those other works that were written to the glory of God. But prayer comes from the lips of ordinary people as well as geniuses. From the lips of children who made sweet hosannas ring, to the works of art of the great masters, come the prayers of the world. It is in this spirit that icon painters pray before they begin work.

In this first part of the hymn Montgomery explores these things: he is feeling his way towards an understanding of what prayer is, and its relationship to the needs of the human spirit. Now he begins to direct the reader's attention to specific situations. Prayer is the 'sound', though it need not be an actual sound, of the sinner repenting: that wonderful moment of insight in which a person suddenly confronts the real self, and sees it for what it is. It is a moment of the rediscovery of the true human being. It is also a moment of goodness, and of God: a moment when 'angels in their songs rejoice', because there is more joy in heaven over one sinner that repents than over 99 that did not go astray. From this point on, prayer is 'the Christian's vital breath', that which keeps him alive. As Peter Baelz wrote in *Does God Answer Prayer?*, without prayer, 'Christian discipleship lapses into moral endeavour.' Here it becomes 'his native air', that which he is accustomed to and breathes naturally. And when it comes to his death, prayer is his watchword, or password, at the gate of heaven.

So the hymn rises to a climax, enumerating the positive virtues of prayer. It unites people in fellowship with God and his Son Jesus Christ; and the Holy Spirit pleads for us, and Jesus intercedes (Montgomery is quoting Romans 8.26 and Hebrews 7.25). Prayer is, as George Herbert put it

> The soul in paraphrase, heart in pilgrimage,
> The Christian plummet sounding heaven and earth;
> Engine against the Almighty, sinner's tower,
> Reversed thunder, Christ-side-piercing spear . . .

This comes from his sonnet 'Prayer (I)', in which Herbert imagines prayer as a kind of weapon against God: a siege engine, a tower for breaching the ramparts, thunder coming back from earth towards heaven, and a spear piercing the side of Christ, from which came blood and water. Herbert's poem is like Montgomery's hymn, but more dramatic; both writers see the importance of prayer as communicating with God. And Montgomery's first verses are an extension of Herbert's suggestion that prayer is 'the soul in paraphrase, heart in pilgrimage'.

The interaction between the human and the divine is beautifully described in the last verse of the hymn. It is addressed to Jesus, who said, 'I am the way, the truth, and the life' (John 14.6), and it reminds us that Jesus himself prayed, most memorably in the Garden of Gethsemane; it ends by incorporating the moment in the lives of the 12 apostles when one of them said, 'Lord, teach us to pray.' What we have learned from this hymn is what is meant in those words: give us, O Lord, not only a form of words but also an expression of our deepest feelings; give us, too, words that are simple, and words that are sublime; give us the words with which to repent; and above all, give us the words which keep us alive. As John Donne, with whom we began, wrote:

> That soul, that is accustomed to direct herself to God, upon every occasion, that, as a flower at sun-rising, conceives a sense of God, in every beam of his, and spreads and dilates itself towards him, in a thankfulness, in every small blessing that he sheds upon her . . . that soul, who, whatsoever string be stricken in her, bass or treble, her high or her low estate, is ever tuned toward God, that soul prays sometimes when it does not know that it prays.

Take my life, and let it be
Frances Ridley Havergal (1836–79)

Take my life, and let it be
Consecrated, Lord, to thee;
Take my moments and my days,
Let them flow in endless praise.

Take my hands, and let them move
At the impulse of thy love;
Take my feet, and let them be
Swift and beautiful for thee.

Take my voice, and let me sing
Always, only, for my King;
Take my lips, and let them be
Filled with messages from thee.

Take my silver and my gold,
Not a mite would I withhold;
Take my intellect, and use
Every power as thou shalt choose.

Take my will, and make it thine;
It shall be no longer mine;
Take my heart: it is thine own;
It shall be thy royal throne.

Take my love; my Lord, I pour
At thy feet its treasure-store;
Take myself, and I will be
Ever, only, all for thee.

Some Victorian women hymn writers suffered from ill health, or
depression, or frustration with their lack of opportunity. Frances
Ridley Havergal was an exception. She was an active, lively, intel-
ligent woman, devout and earnest as a child, with a personality

that delighted all who knew her. An Irish girl who met her in 1856, when Frances was 19, said that when she came into the room she 'flashed in like a burst of sunshine, like a hillside breeze'. She was a remarkable linguist, speaking French and German fluently, and studying Latin, Greek and Hebrew; she was a very good musician, a fine pianist with a beautiful singing voice; and she was athletic and bold, a good swimmer and a mountaineer, climbing in the Alps 'midway between heaven and earth' as she put it (she was nearly killed once, glissading down).

Her father was a Worcestershire clergyman, and she grew up in a religious home, seeking earnestly for an assurance of the love of God in Christ. When she found that assurance, on Advent Sunday 1873, she wrote rapturously of her new life, and thereafter sought to influence others to trust in God: 'The really leaving *everything* to Him is so inexpressibly sweet, and surely He does arrange so much better than we could for ourselves, when we leave it all to Him.' But she caught typhoid fever in 1874, and was never very strong again, dying at the age of 42.

The *Memorials of Frances Ridley Havergal*, consisting largely of her own letters, were edited by her sister Maria. On the front cover were reproduced the first two lines of this hymn, which was originally written in two-line verses. It is a hymn of dedication written by an ardent and loving spirit, and it has continued to move its readers because of the unreserved self-giving that it demonstrates. Couplet after couplet surrenders different aspects of her life to Christ, whom she called 'my King', 'my Master', 'my Lord'. At the same time, each couplet is a prayer, so that the hymn is a devotional exercise, comparable to those of a postulant entering a nunnery, or of a candidate for ordination. Either might be moved to pray, in the words of the first couplet, for the future to be 'consecrated' – set apart for a religious purpose.

'Consecrated', coming as it does after the simple first line, has a wonderful resonance here. The voice savours the long word and dwells upon it after the monosyllables of the first line. It is full of meaning. We speak of 'consecrated ground', such as churchyards, or of a 'consecration' of a bishop, meaning that they are set apart for sacred purposes. Frances Ridley Havergal is here praying to be set apart, as a priest might be, although she could not have been a priest in the nineteenth century; nevertheless she could still pray to dedicate herself to God. The word she uses, at the beginning of every couplet, is 'take': 'Take my life', 'Take my moments', 'Take my hands', 'Take my feet', 'Take my intellect'. One by one her brilliant talents are laid before Christ. She had hands which played the piano superbly, Beethoven and Mendelssohn especially; she had feet which were capable of athletic and adventurous Alpine walking; she had a voice which enchanted all who heard it, but which she decided to devote to the singing of sacred music only. She had lips, by which she spoke to others, and converted them; she had money, which she spent for Christ; and she had a fine intellect which was capable of mastering foreign languages and of writing poetry. Finally in the hymn she ceases to enumerate specific talents, and turns to the entire self: will, heart, love and finally 'myself', the whole person, complete.

For most people this is a hymn of the highest aspiration, one which may be sung with an uneasy feeling that such high ideals are hard to live up to. Yet we can pray to do so, pray that God will take such talents that we have and use them. In this context, the couplet which has always caused the greatest problems is

> Take my silver and my gold;
> Not a mite would I withhold.

But Frances Ridley Havergal's own comment on it helps to answer the criticisms. She thought that it was 'peculiarly liable to be objected to by those who do not really understand the *spirit* of it', and went on, quoting the 'not a mite' line:

> that does not mean that, because we have ten shillings in our purse, we are pledged to put it *all* in the next collecting plate, else we should have none for the next call! But it does mean that every shilling is to be, and I think I may say *is*, held at my Lord's disposal, and is distinctly not my own; but, as He has entrusted to me a body for my special charge, I am bound to clothe that body with His silver and gold, so that it shall neither suffer from cold, nor bring discredit upon His cause! I still forget sometimes, but as a rule I never spend a sixpence without the distinct feeling that it is His, and must be spent for Him only, even if indirectly.

Money is not to be hoarded, but used, and used responsibly. The common sense which this displays is part of Frances Ridley Havergal's very attractive personality. She was obviously a woman who gladdened all hearts, and who enlivened all around her. But she was also dedicated to living for her 'Master'. Her 'consecration hymn' is a full expression of her zeal, and it is significant that it was written in January 1874, about a month after her great experience on Advent Sunday 1873.

It is also an expansion of the words which she would have said, Sunday by Sunday, at Holy Communion. When it was first published in her poetry book called *Loyal Responses*, this hymn was prefaced by the words: 'Here we offer and present unto Thee, O Lord, ourselves, our souls and bodies, to be a reasonable, holy, and lively sacrifice unto Thee.' Whenever we say these words, we should think of the way in which the service of Holy Communion challenges us as well as comforts us, asks us to dedicate ourselves anew to the service of Christ.

Her own life was an example of those words put into practice. She possessed wonderful talents, and had great abilities. At the same time she had all the disadvantages of being a woman in the nineteenth century; but she lived life to the full, and clearly enriched the lives of all who knew her. Her hymn is an inspiration to all who would follow her example.

Teach me, my God and King
George Herbert (1593–1633)

Teach me, my God and King,
In all things thee to see;
And what I do in any thing
To do it as for thee.

A man that looks on glass,
On it may stay his eye;
Or if he pleaseth, through it pass,
And then the heaven espy.

All may of thee partake;
Nothing can be so mean,
Which with this tincture, 'for thy sake',
Will not grow bright and clean.

A servant with this clause
Makes drudgery divine;
Who sweeps a room, as for thy laws,
Makes that and the action fine.

This is the famous stone
That turneth all to gold;
For that which God doth touch and own
Cannot for less be told.

Some hymns begin on earth and take us up to heaven, both in
what they say (as in 'Love divine, all loves excelling') and in the
way in which they inspire us as we sing, so that we begin the
hymn in a normal earthbound state and end it in a thrilling vision
of a purer and better world. This one does something different. It
is about work, and it reflects on the place of work in the Christian
life. *Laborare est orare*, 'to work is to pray', was the saying of the
monks in the Middle Ages; this hymn explores that idea in a more

complicated way, but one which makes us understand better what is involved in uniting the concerns of our everyday life with our duty to God.

It was written by George Herbert, the son of a famous family who was destined for great prosperity (he came to the attention of James I when he was Public Orator at Cambridge) but who gave it up to become a country clergyman at Bemerton, near Salisbury. There he lived an exemplary life of a country parson for a few years, before his untimely death at the age of 39; according to his biographer, Isaak Walton, he lived and died like a saint, 'unspotted of the World, full of Alms-deeds, full of Humility, and all the examples of a virtuous life'. Shortly before his death he sent a manuscript of his poems to his friend Nicholas Ferrar, with the words:

> Tell him, he shall find in it a picture of the many spiritual Conflicts that have past betwixt God and my soul, before I could subject mine to the will of *Jesus my Master*: in whose service I have now found perfect freedom; desire him to read it: and then, if he can think it may turn to the advantage of any dejected poor Soul, let it be made publick: if not, let him burn it: for *I and it, are less than the least of God's mercies.*

Fortunately Ferrar did not burn the manuscript, but sent it to Cambridge to be printed; and since that time it has guided many people though periods of uncertainty and doubt, and shown them something of the loveliness and beauty of the spiritual life. The book was called *The Temple*: this poem from it was called 'The Elixir', which refers to the medieval practice of alchemy. During the Middle Ages alchemists sought perpetually for what was called the 'philosopher's stone' or 'the elixir', a substance which would turn base metals into gold, and therefore make the possessor uniquely rich and powerful.

This unworthy aim is taken up by Herbert and used to indicate a spiritual state. There *is* an elixir, something which will turn our lives into gold: it is to see God in all things, and to do all things for God. If we do that, then our lives will be transformed. Just as the base metals might be turned into gold by the alchemists' elixir, so our ordinary lives can be turn into golden or blessed ones by the presence of God.

We do this in two ways: by 'seeing' God in everything, and by 'doing' all things in that frame of mind. So the poem begins with a prayer to 'my God and King' for these two things. The second verse uses a homely image to illustrate what 'seeing' God might mean: we can look at a window and see the window itself, or we can look through it to see the sky beyond. So in our everyday lives we can see things as they are, material things (fields, trees, hills, people), or we can see them with eyes that see in them 'heaven', the spiritual quality that exists everywhere if only we could be brought to see it. If we begin to see the whole world as suffused with the presence of God, then it, and we, will be transformed.

Everything can be treated this way, says Herbert: 'All may of thee partake.' Even the meanest object can be made 'bright and clean' if we see it this way. Now he uses images of cleaning: we all know that a grubby object can be made more attractive by washing or polishing, especially if we have the right kind of detergent or polish. Herbert's polish has a name: it is called 'For thy sake'. It is as though he takes a bottle or tin labelled 'For thy sake' and applies the liquid to the dirty surface. This is connected with the elixir idea, because the elixir was sometimes called the 'universal tincture', something which would transform an object into something infinitely more precious. He then imagines servants doing the cleaning: if they sweep the room 'with this clause' ('For thy sake'), then the room will be fine (clean) and the action will be fine (good) too. Two things happen at once: the room is transformed, and the work is transformed also. Even drudgery, the most dull but unavoidable labour, can become divine.

And so the poem sums up everything in the last verse: 'This is the famous stone.' We might put it more emphatically: '*This* is the famous stone.' This is the secret that philosophers and alchemists spent their lives searching for, and which sometimes drove them mad. Their obsession with finding the philosopher's stone appears ridiculous when placed beside Herbert's simple solution: the presence of God is what will turn all to gold. It is that which will transform our lives, and our work. It will give meaning to work, and beauty to life: everywhere, even within our own selves, the tincture will make thoughts and lives bright and clean. If God 'touches' this life, and 'owns' it (approves it), then it is truly the stone itself.

It is a common saying, that we are 'servants of God'. Herbert's poem assures us that such a service is indeed, as he said in the letter to Nicholas Ferrar, 'perfect freedom', the transformation of life from the world of materialism and the self to the world of the spirit and of God. We can see the glass, or we can see the heaven behind it: the choice is ours. But Herbert makes it very clear that the right choice is the one that he had made himself: to see God in everything and to do everything for God. That way, life becomes really, properly, enduringly golden.

The poem is not an easy one, and if it is to be understood correctly it requires explanations from alchemical history and a knowledge of the vocabulary involved. But since its first printing as a hymn in the *English Hymnal* of 1906 it has become a firm favourite. This is because, underneath the complex language and the compressed lines, we recognize the simplicity of what Herbert is saying: that life is better when it is not lived selfishly, that work is better when it is done in the right spirit rather than grudgingly, that dirt *can* be removed and an object *can* be made clean, even if that object is a sinful self. It is a poem which brilliantly combines common sense, human experience and hope.

Lord, for the years your love has kept and guided

Timothy Dudley-Smith (born 1926)

———◆◆◆———

Lord, for the years your love has kept and guided,
   urged and inspired us, cheered us on our way,
sought us and saved us, pardoned and provided,
   Lord of the years, we bring our thanks today.

Lord, for that word, the word of life which fires us,
   speaks to our hearts and sets our souls ablaze,
teaches and trains, rebukes us and inspires us,
   Lord of the word, receive your people's praise.

Lord, for our land, in this our generation,
   spirits oppressed by pleasure, wealth and care;
for young and old, for commonwealth and nation,
   Lord of our land, be pleased to hear our prayer.

Lord, for our world; when we disown and doubt him,
   loveless in strength, and comfortless in pain;
hungry and helpless, lost indeed without him,
   Lord of the world, we pray that Christ may reign.

Lord, for ourselves; in living power remake us,
   self on the cross and Christ upon the throne;
past put behind us, for the future take us,
   Lord of our lives, to live for Christ alone.

Timothy Dudley-Smith, who was Bishop of Thetford before his
retirement, is the best-known living British hymn writer. His 'Tell
out, my soul, the greatness of the Lord', written in 1961, was one
of the first new hymns written after the Second World War to
become widely known and popular. It was followed by others,
notably Sydney Carter's 'Lord of the Dance' (if that can be called

a hymn rather than a song). But 'Tell out my soul' was the one that showed the others the way. It was written as a poem rather than a hymn, based on a quotation which Dudley-Smith had read in a review of the *New English Bible New Testament*. It came from the first chapter of St Luke's Gospel (verse 46), in which the Virgin Mary gives thanks to God in the hymn that we call the Magnificat; these words gave that ancient hymn a new life in contemporary language.

It was a poem, according to the author, because 'at that time I believed that hymn writing was closed to me because I lack all musical ability'. Fortunately its success encouraged him to write many more: there are no fewer than 285 in *A House of Praise*, his collected hymns from 1961 to 2001. The present one dates from 1967. It was written at the request of the Scripture Union to mark their centenary, and it was sung on that occasion in St Paul's Cathedral to the tune Finlandia. It then had a fine tune written for it by Michael Baughen: since that time it has almost always been set to that tune, which is called Lord of the Years.

It is a fine hymn for a centenary, but it can be used to mark any special occasion, especially if that occasion is one on which the congregation is looking back with thankfulness. It was sung, for example, at many services in 1995 to mark the fiftieth anniversary of the end of the Second World War. From the marvellous first line onwards – Timothy Dudley-Smith has the knack of writing arresting first lines – the hymn expresses what many people feel as they look back over the years: that there has been some kind of providence at work, for which our hearts must be, as the General Thanksgiving puts it, 'unfeignedly thankful':

> We thine unworthy servants do give thee most humble and hearty thanks for all thy goodness and loving-kindness to us, and to all men; We bless thee for our creation, preservation, and all the blessings of this life; but above all, for thine inestimable love in the redemption of the world by our Lord Jesus Christ; for the means of grace, and for the hope of glory.

The first verse of this hymn follows the same pattern of thankfulness but in a new language: we have been kept and guided, urged on and inspired, cheered on our way, sought and saved, pardoned and provided for. The verbs succeed each other very powerfully, one after another like waves, to lay out the pattern of creation and preservation, blessing and redemption. By the end of it the singer is overwhelmed by the sense of a spiritual good fortune, bringing thanks to this day; that is, bringing to this moment and this place the sense of all those accumulated years, with all their blessings. In the memory the past lies before us, brought forward and presented with gratitude at the feet of God.

The second verse gives thanks for the Holy Scripture, which is a reminder of the occasion for which the hymn was written. But the verse transcends that 1967 service, of course: the continuing relevance of the Bible to our lives must always be a source of strength. As Anne Steele, the eighteenth-century Baptist hymn writer wrote:

> Father of mercies, in thy word
> What endless glory shines!
> For ever be thy name adored
> For these celestial lines.

In the present hymn, the Bible is just such an 'endless glory'. It is 'the word of life' which inspires us, educates us, corrects us, and speaks to our hearts. But perhaps because the Bible itself is a book about the good society as well as the individual spiritual experience, the hymn moves out from ourselves (verse 1) and our inspiration (verse 2) into our world. The third verse remembers our, or any, land in which the quest for material wealth and worldly goods has destroyed the spiritual life. 'Getting and spending', Wordsworth called it:

> The World is too much with us; late and soon,
> Getting and spending, we lay waste our powers . . .

This verse echoes that sentiment. It is one of the most effective modern hymns that approaches the problems of a modern secular society, preoccupied with the pursuit of pleasure and the glorification of wealth: this one sums up the problems ('oppressed by pleasure' is particularly neat) followed by a prayer for the commonwealth and nation. This is not, I think, the 'Commonwealth', the loose union of states following the dispersal of the British Empire, but the 'commonwealth', what used to be called 'the common weal', the ideal society to which each person contributes a necessary part. The verse is a reminder, not only of our tendency to secularism and materialism, but also of our responsibility to one another. Good societies are made up of good people.

And from the ideal of nationhood as a responsible and Christian commonwealth, the fourth verse moves out still further to the world. It is a world in which many are hungry and helpless; it is a world in which Christ is disowned and doubted, in spite of his sufferings for mankind. With a glance at the Passion of Christ, 'loveless in strength, and comfortless in pain', we are reminded to 'pray that Christ may reign', that his love and forgiving mercy may be a part of the global recognition of human need. Those who care for the poor in the streets of Calcutta, those who work as doctors or teachers or helpers in lands where ignorance is common, those who work through diplomacy and politics to try to make a fairer economic world, all these and many others testify to a modern kind of missionary work, which is summed up in the last line of this verse: 'Lord of the world, we pray that Christ may reign.'

But occasions such as the one for which this hymn was written are not just for looking back and celebrating. Properly used, they should look forward as well as back. Commemoration should not be just a matter of thankfulness for the past, but of dedication for the future. And so, with a grand inevitability, the hymn comes round to ourselves: from the world we turn finally to our own future, praying to be remade in living power. The last verse is one in which we turn away from ourselves and to the values that are exemplified in the life and teaching of Jesus Christ. As the second line puts it, the self is 'on the cross', which is a reworking of Galatians 6.14, which glories in the cross of Christ, 'by whom the world is crucified unto me, and I unto the world'. That verse, which was also the inspiration for Isaac Watts's 'When I survey the wondrous cross', here reminds us of the need, as we contemplate the past, to dedicate ourselves to Christ in the future: 'past put behind us, for the future take us'. The accumulated thankfulness gives way to the promise of action. In that way, our gratitude for all the blessings of this life will not be expressed in prayer only: it will be transformed into a better future for ourselves and for our fellow human beings.